#WINNING

Wisdom for God's Warriors

CODI GANDEE

WESTBOW
PRESS®
A DIVISION OF THOMAS NELSON
& ZONDERVAN

Scripture taken from the King James Version of the Bible.

WestBow Press books may be ordered through booksellers or by contacting:

WestBow Press
A Division of Thomas Nelson & Zondervan
1663 Liberty Drive
Bloomington, IN 47403
www.westbowpress.com
1 (866) 928-1240

ISBN: 978-1-9736-0687-1 (sc)
ISBN: 978-1-9736-0688-8 (e)

Library of Congress Control Number: 2017916603

Print information available on the last page.

WestBow Press rev. date: 10/25/2017

CONTENTS

ACKNOWLEDGMENTS

Dad and Mom, Cass, Jeffrey, Cade and Jake, Tim and Kayla, Pam, Rick and Rebecca, thank you for your help, support and encouragement. I love you all.

Sadi, Chlo and Zeke, your daddy and I would pick you every time. We love you.

Trae Gandee, you are my dream come true. You are the answer to the prayers I didn't know to pray. I am head over heels in love with you HM.

Jesus, without you I am nothing. Thank you for your grace and guidance. Use me and all that I do for your glory. I am yours.

BECOMING A CHRISTIAN

- Realize that you are a sinner. "For all have sinned, and come short of the glory of God;" Romans 3:23
- Acknowledge that there is a penalty for the sins you commit. "For the wages of sin is death; but the gift of God is eternal life through Jesus Christ our Lord." Romans 6:23
- Believe that Jesus paid the price for your sins by dying on the cross and that he rose from the grave. "Who was delivered for our offenses, and was raised again for our justification." Romans 4:25
- Ask the Lord to forgive you of your sin and he will. "That if thou shalt confess with thy mouth the Lord Jesus, and shalt believe in thine heart that God hath raised him from the dead, thou shalt be saved." Romans 10:9
- Get to know Jesus. Study the Word! "In the beginning was the Word and the Word was with God, and the Word was God." John 1:1

INTRODUCTION

What exactly is wisdom? How can I get it? How long before I can get it? Where can I get it from? Is it possible that I already have it?

Jesus tells us very plainly in Matthew 7:7-8, "Ask, and it shall be given you; seek, and ye shall find; knock, and it shall be opened unto you: For every one that asketh receiveth; and he that seeketh findeth; and to him that knocketh it shall be opened."

So I went to the Lord. "Please, Lord, show me what wisdom is. Let me obtain it. I want it for myself. I want it for other Christians. I know that with your wisdom we can have a great impact on your church, on the legacies that we leave behind. Teach me, teach us your ways."

When I surrendered to write this study, I knew there wasn't any way that I could condense God's wisdom into a sixteen lesson study guide. I prayed that the Lord would show me a passage of scripture that would help us as we seek to be wise warriors. If you'll notice, the first lesson of each chapter is based on David's results of walking wisely in the Lord as recorded in I Samuel 18:5-30. This scripture is the basis for #winning.

CHAPTER ONE

The Battle Plan

"Fight the good fight of faith, lay hold on eternal life, whereunto thou art called, and hast professed a good profession before many witnesses." I Timothy 6:12

Our time on earth is spent on the spiritual battlefield. Knowing this may help us to understand that our decisions aren't just impactful for us but also for the kingdom we are fighting for. We know best how to battle when we know where to turn for direction.

Lesson One: Living On a Spiritual Battlefield

"Wisdom is better than weapons of war: but one sinner destroyeth much good." Ecclesiastes 9:18

Either you are fighting for Jesus or you are fighting for the adversary. Accepting this truth allows you to better grasp an underlying theme of the Word: the choices before us are polar opposites.

In Romans 7 we are given a law: when we purpose to do good, evil is present with us. In Ephesians 6 the Word states what that "evil" is: not flesh and blood, but principalities, powers, rulers of the darkness of the world, spiritual wickedness in high places. Essentially we wrestle against the deceit of the devil.

One of the tactics Satan often tries to use is to persuade us that we aren't actually in a battle. He attempts to blind us to the need of giving ourselves completely to Christ. Jesus addresses the lie in Luke 11:23. He says "He that is not with me is against me: and he that gathereth not with me scattereth." To not be completely devoted to Jesus is to surrender to the scheme of Satan.

We are told to walk in the light as opposed to the darkness (Ephesians 5:8). We are reminded of the differences between sweet water and bitter (James 3:11). We are given the opportunity to choose life and good over death and evil (Deuteronomy 30:15).

True wisdom has an opposite too: a devilish one. The book of James teaches on the difference between the two.

Read James 3:13-17. What is within the heart of an unwise person?

What are the results of that person's choices?

What are the traits of heavenly wisdom?

Read Proverbs 1:20-23. This passage of scripture seems to beg us to attain wisdom. It says for us to simply turn to it and wisdom will be poured out upon us.

Read Proverbs 2:1-6. Remember the words of Christ? Ask and you will receive, knock and it will be opened, seek and you will find? Wisdom isn't illusive to the child of God but we must open ourselves to receiving it.

Believe what the Word says to be true. Think on the truths within it. Listen for the Lord to speak to you. Study the Word. Ask for knowledge. Ask for understanding. Be willing to learn. Jesus will give you wisdom.

Read Proverbs 3:13-18. List the benefits of obtaining wisdom.

The scriptures, through the Holy Spirit, enlighten us. It is through them that we learn how to become more like Christ. It is in the Word that we find hope and life eternal.

Prayerfully consider how you may benefit from seeking wisdom. What is the Lord speaking to you through these few scriptures?

In John 21 Jesus asked Peter three different times "Peter, do you love me?" Three different times Peter said "Yes." Jesus responded each time with, "Feed my sheep". Jesus wanted Peter to show him that he loved him, not just tell him. Of course God can read our hearts; he knows all, but the people of this world, including ourselves, benefit when we back up our good intentions with actions. Instead of just saying "I want wisdom" validate your words by asking for it. Search for wisdom. Listen for Jesus to speak it you, to show you what wisdom is.

Here are a couple of scripture references to get you started on your search for wisdom:

"In all thy ways acknowledge him, and he shall direct thy paths." Proverbs 3:6

We can put this scripture to action by praying a simple prayer. For example: Lord, I need you to lead me in the decision I need to make today.

"Commit thy works unto the Lord, and thy thoughts shall be established." Proverbs 16:3

Again, praying something similar to "Lord, I am going to do this for your glory" invites the Lord to bless your work for the Lord.

What are you going to do to show him that you are serious about gaining wisdom?

I encourage you to put forth the effort to obtain wisdom because a person that finds and adheres to the wisdom from the Word is a person that is ready for spiritual battle. They are a person that is #winning at life.

Meeting One: The Battle Plan

"Fight the good fight of faith, lay hold on eternal life, whereunto thou art called, and hast professed a good profession before many witnesses." I Timothy 6:12

Living On a Spiritual Battlefield

Ultimately our respect for the Lord begins when we realize our need for him and then accept him as our Savior. This is when our first wise choice is made. As Christians we have chosen the Lord as opposed to believing the lie.

My dad and mom raised me in a Christian home. I have attended church all of my life. I was given a solid foundation to build upon. I knew that I didn't have a terrible past. Also I realized that I wouldn't have a great future if I didn't have Christ. I was able to understand that Jesus was my only hope. I was eight years old when I accepted Jesus as my Savior.

Share with the group your salvation story; the time in which you first obtained a heavenly wisdom.

The enemy is real but so is the Victor. You are on the battlefield as a soldier of the Most High God. Wise warriors of the Lord know how to interact with their God and their fellow soldiers. In the Chapter Two: Peaceful Relationships, we will study the benefits of cultivating God-glorifying relationships in our life. Walking in the wisdom of the Lord strengthens our relationship with other Christians. Jesus embraced relationships. We are going to study how we should be doing the same.

CHAPTER TWO

Peaceful Relationships

"And we beseech you, brethren, to know them which labour among you, and are over you in the Lord, and admonish you; And to esteem them very highly in love for their work's sake. And be at peace among yourselves." I Thessalonians 5:12-13

Lesson Two: Promises of Peace

Peace is evident when we begin our walk with Christ. We have obtained peace because it is a fruit of the Spirit that lives within us (Galatians 5:22). Jesus, our Lord, is known as the Prince of Peace (Isaiah 9:6).

Does conflict sometimes surface in our day to day life? Yes. Will we face hard times? Yes. Jesus teaches that the sun will rise on the evil and the good and that it rains on the just and unjust (Matthew 5:45). We will face afflictions but we can still rest in the peace of God (I Thessalonians 3:3). The difference between "the evil" and "the good" is that we, "the good", have surrendered our lives to God, the author of peace (I Corinthians 14:33).

Considering these facts, we can conclude that peace isn't a result of an absence of conflict. Instead, peace is a constant in our lives when we live in the will of our Savior. Philippians 4:7 says that our peace is "the peace of God, which passeth all understanding". It cannot be measured by the standards of this world.

The peace that we gain from having a relationship with Christ can be found trickling into our other relationships as well. If we seek wisdom, eventually the Lord will show us to do as the Word says in Psalm 34:14 and "depart from evil, and do good; seek peace, and pursue it".

Most usually, acting wisely in our relationship with Christ will lead to our relationships with others benefiting. At worst, conflicts that arise can still result in the peace of God for us, if for no one else.

Wisdom Leads to Peace

Read I Samuel 17:32-51.

David, a young shepherd had a personal relationship with God. Because this relationship existed, we know that David possessed at least the beginning of wisdom. David wisely relied upon God to protect him from the dangers that he would face. He looked to God for protection of his father's livelihood. David had courageously rescued his father's livestock from a lion and a bear because he trusted that God would be with him. In the history of their relationship, David had never seen the Lord forsake him. In our own relationship and history with God, we can always see our God as faithful. This is an encouragement to us as we continue to press on.

We are told to record the good that God has done in our lives so that when hard times come our way, we have strength (I Timothy 6:19). Record some of the high points of your history that you can look to for encouragement to go forward.

David was also able to look back and see God as faithful to him. Their relationship grew to be one of complete trust and respect. David was so confident in his God's ability that he didn't hesitate to willingly battle against the enemy's champion, Goliath.

Goliath, however, was disgusted that David would attempt to fight him. He insulted David. He cursed him. He boasted what he would do with David once he won the war. He took his opponent lightly. In this, Goliath made a fatal mistake.

Occasionally on this spiritual battlefield we find ourselves in the enemy's territory. We get into this position either when we minimize the evil of this world and the intent of Satan or we put too much confidence in ourselves and quit relying on the strength of the Lord. Carelessness and pride are dangerous characteristics to go into battle with. For us, it is so important to be sober and vigilant because our adversary the devil walks around as a roaring lion seeking whom he may devour (I Peter 5:8).

David responded to the taunts of Goliath with the same wisdom that we have offered to us today:

David acknowledged the weapons of Goliath as legitimate. David said, "You have a sword, a spear and a shield". He named what he was up against. It is so much easier to battle if you recognize the weapons that are being used against you and who it is at the root of the attack.

Take time to evaluate what you are battling against and record it.

David learned the battlefield. He knew not to get within arm's length of Goliath. He understood that it was most likely that his flesh could not sustain a fatal hit from the Goliath's sword. In Romans 14, we are warned to not put a stumbling block or an occasion to fall in the way of our fellow Christians. If we are to know what may be harmful to our spiritual brethren then it stands to reason that we should be able to acknowledge what may cause our own selves to waiver. Learn your weaknesses and then draw a line. Don't put yourself in a position where you are likely to fail.

Ask the Lord to show you where to put up your boundary line(s). Write your plan down in the space below.

David made known that he was fighting for our Lord. "I come to you in the name of our Lord. The battle is the Lord's and he will give you into our hands." He didn't say, "You haven't seen me with a slingshot, Goliath". He made the battle about the Lord, not himself. When we pause to think about whom we are representing, the battle doesn't seem nearly as daunting.

Just as important as knowing what he was up against and where his strength lay, David knew how to use the weapon he had been given. He had proved the slingshot and stones. He knew, from experience, that what the Lord had equipped him with was enough to walk away unharmed. Know your weapon: the Word, the sword of the Spirit (Ephesians 6:17). John 1:1 says "In the beginning was the Word, and the Word was with God, and the Word was God." If you want assurance that you aren't battling alone, take the Word with you. Study it. Meditate upon it. Learn it. Memorize it. Hide it in your heart.

Find scripture that speaks to your current battle. Write it down and memorize it.

Finally, as David stood before the giant he claimed the victory with a peace that passed all understanding. He then ran towards Goliath, faced him head on and flung the stone at just the right time. You never have to fear Satan if you are standing with Jesus. There is absolutely zero reason to cower or hide. You are a soldier of Jesus Christ (II Timothy 2:3).

David won the battle every time, just the same as you and I will if we rely on the wisdom of God. David also remained peaceful in his relationship with God in the midst of the most significant conflict he had ever faced. King Saul took notice of David's composure. He recognized David as someone that his kingdom could benefit from. He chose to continue to use David in wartime because he wanted to capitalize on the wisdom and the peace that David possessed. Jesus sees that same potential in you. He has given you wisdom and peace. He knows you are capable of living the gospel that he has called you to preach (Philippians 4:13). The Lord has set you up to succeed. You make the decision of how you will respond.

This passage of scripture is just the beginning of David's story as a chosen vessel of God. He was continually faced with making decisions.

Read I Samuel 18:5. How did David conduct himself? What was the result of that?

David's wisdom, stemming from his relationship with the Lord, led to peaceful relationships with an entire nation of people. But more important than popularity with the majority was David's knowledge that he walked wisely before his Lord.

In what ways has obtaining the peace of God affected you?

How has this led you to make decisions that are wise in the Lord?

Peace was a constant with David because of his relationship with God. David was able to recognize his battle and the tactics the enemy would use against him. He knew that to be victorious he had to have the Lord with him.

Lesson Three: Christian Camaraderie

"Let brotherly love continue." Hebrews 13:1

David the Warrior later became known as King David of Israel, a person forever recorded in the Word as a man after God's own heart (Acts 13:22). He was also the father to Solomon, the king made famous because of his wisdom (I Kings 4:34). In this lesson we will be studying Solomon's wisdom during his transitioning years as he prepares to step in as king and begin rule over the nation chosen by God.

Wise Mature Christians Invest in Inexperienced Christians

Read I Chronicles 22:1-16.

David had his mind set on building a house for the Ark of the Covenant to dwell. He set out to do this but the Lord wouldn't bless it. David had been a man of war, a man that had shed blood. The Lord wanted a man of peace to build his house. The Lord ordained Solomon to build the temple instead.

David was faced with a decision. Would he go against the Lord and begin constructing a temple or would he submit to the Lord's plan of using Solomon to build the house of God? David, in his wisdom, chose to adhere to God's plan. However, he didn't turn his back on his dream and his son. Instead, David began to invest in both the temple and Solomon.

The passion to see God glorified led David to hire masons to hew the stones that would later be used for the building. He had iron stored up to be used as nails and joints. He made sure that brass was plentiful and Cedar wood was in abundance. The amount of gold and silver that had been laid up couldn't be numbered. Laborers were standing ready; waiting for the command to get to work.

The preparations David made for his son's future are the embodiment of wisdom from the Lord. David cared so greatly for Solomon and his future that he willingly invested his own time, effort and resources to see that Solomon had the best opportunity to fulfill the calling on his life.

David's choice to help prepare Solomon, his successor, is an example of how the family of God should work. Mature Christians should be willing, ready and looking for opportunities to invest in Christians that are in the beginning stages of their walk with Christ. What that looks like varies from situation to situation. For Abraham it was giving Lot the first option of the fields (Genesis 13:1-11). For Paul it was allowing Timothy to accompany him on missionary trips (Act 16:1-3).

What are some other ways that mature Christians can help to prepare inexperienced Christians as they move forward?

Not only did David show Solomon that he was investing in his future by making the supplies available to build the temple, but he also spoke words of encouragement to him. He gave Solomon instruction that he could reference for strength and guidance.

David was sure to mention that wisdom and understanding only came from the Lord. This advice reminded Solomon that no person, including himself, is wiser than the Lord. Understanding that God knows all and sees all not only keeps us in awe of our Savior but it also keeps us coming to him for guidance and direction.

David reminded Solomon of the calling the Lord had put on his life: to govern Israel and to keep the law of the Lord thy God. When we are working with someone we need to keep the goal in mind: you are helping this person to follow Jesus. It isn't necessary for you to know what the calling on their life is; it may not even be made known to them yet. Regardless, our position should be the same: to encourage them to keep making decisions to actively follow after the Lord.

David concludes his charge by telling him that he will prosper if he follows God. We will prosper also if we look to Jesus to direct our paths; if we remember that following him is what this life is all about.

If you were given an opportunity to tell someone what they should do as they mature in Christ what would you say?

Wise Inexperienced Christians Mirror the Mature Christians

Despite everything that David had poured into his son and his future, Solomon was still responsible for his own choices. David could point him to the path of righteousness but Solomon had to make the decision to walk down it.

The time had come for Solomon to make a decision without his father there to guide him. This is the time that David had prepared Solomon for. If Solomon is to act wisely, he will remember the wise words and examples of his father.

Read I Kings 3:5-14.

"For this cause also thank we God without ceasing, because, when ye received the word of God which ye heard of us, ye received it not as the word of men, but as it is in truth, the word of God, which effectually worketh also in you that believe." I Thessalonians 2:13

God said to Solomon, "Ask what I shall give thee." Solomon's response was one of a person that was wise in the ways of the Lord. He began by acknowledging God as merciful and the one in control. He praised God for the kindness that had been shown to his father. We learn that Solomon had observed his father, his mentor, because he was able to recount the highpoints of his father's life. Solomon then recalled his father's words "only the Lord give thee wisdom and understanding". He asked the Lord to bless him with wisdom so that he could rightly judge the great people of Israel.

Solomon's answer gives us insight into the type of man that Solomon was. He was one to humble himself before God. He hadn't turned a deaf ear to his father's advice. He not only listened to David, but he also watched his father make decisions and learned from them. Solomon knew that his father gave up his own desires in order to submit to the Lord. Solomon chose to make the Lord's calling on his life the number one priority too. Solomon wasn't concerned with wealth or longevity. He was consumed with the desire to please the Lord. He wanted to rule God's people justly, first and foremost.

Write out Matthew 6:33.

In what ways are you deliberately choosing to seek God before all else?

God was so pleased with Solomon's response that he blessed him with wisdom. After that blessing God continued to add to it. Next, he received riches. Then, he was blessed with honor. If Solomon would continue to follow after the law of the Lord, God said he would add long life too. The blessings started being poured out upon Solomon when he chose to ask for wisdom. Blessings are poured out upon us when we begin fearing the Lord and begin walking in wisdom. Wisdom is part of the foundation that we build our lives upon.

Seeking Fellow Soldiers

Read 1 Kings 5:1-12.

As Solomon's God-given wisdom was gaining fame throughout the world, so was his kingdom. He was building a temple for the Lord. Solomon wanted to carry on his father's choice to use only the finest materials for the house of God. He too had to look outside his country to continue to obtain the best selection. Choosing the correct trade partners was critical to Solomon's project.

King Hiram of Tyre had been a business partner of David's. They had shared a favorable relationship. Hiram, being made aware that Solomon now reigned in his father's place, recognized the fact that Solomon would be the one that he would have to deal with. Hiram could have responded to the regime change by taking advantage of this new ruler. He could have increased the price of the timber. He could have dealt dishonestly with him. But Hiram chose to treat Solomon with the same respect that he wanted to be treated with (Matthew 7:12). He let Solomon know that he would be available to work with his kingdom, just as he had been there for David.

Solomon could have rejected Hiram's kindness. He could have decided to cut ties with all of David's former partners to show the world that he could make it on his own. But Solomon was wise. He knew of the relationship that Hiram and his father had established. He saw Hiram as someone he could trust. He chose to embrace a relationship with Hiram by suggesting that he continue to supply the wood needed for the building of the temple.

1 Kings 5:7 records that Hiram responded to Solomon's decision by rejoicing and saying

"Blessed be the Lord this day, which hath given unto David a wise son over this great people." He accepted the offer Solomon made. The men worked well together. A peaceable league between the two countries was formed.

"Two are better than one; because they have a good reward for their labour. For if they fall, the one will lift up his fellow: but woe to him that is alone when he falleth; for he hath not another to help him up." Ecclesiastes 4:9-10

Surrounding yourself with people that are working toward the same goal is wisdom. These people will care about your end result because they want the same for themselves. Strengthening the relationships we have with other Christians should be a priority. These people have the same intent as we should have: to see God's kingdom grow and Jesus glorified. They should also be the ones to offer us counsel and encouragement that is based on the Word. Wisdom is investing in Godly relationships.

Who is someone that you are able to confidently look to when seeking wisdom from the Lord?

The Word is full of people from both sides of the battlefield. We can learn from their wisdom or lack thereof. The next couple of lessons we will be studying how Jesus approached an array of relationships while he walked this earth.

Lesson Four: Following Your Commander

"For what is your life? It is even a vapour, that appeareth for a little time, and then vanisheth away." James 4:14

The choices we make in this short period of time have eternal consequences. Life on earth isn't a trial run. Therefore, no battle should be taken lightly or be fought without guidance from our Lord. To make wise decisions, our eyes need to be completely focused on the things of Christ. Walking around blindly causes us to fall (Matthew 15:14). Lacking a vision causes people to perish (Proverbs 29:18). To keep our spiritual vision in focus, our eyes need to be enlightened. This enlightenment comes from obtaining a spirit of wisdom and a spiritual understanding of the Word and causes us to know the hope of Christ's purpose, the riches of Jesus and the greatness of the power of our God (Ephesians 1:17-19).

Enlightened Eyes

A warrior goes to battle with an end result in mind. Successful warriors go in knowing their purpose, with a glimpse of what a victory could bring and willing to use whatever strength they have to achieve it.

Read Ephesians 2:12-18.

Not only is Jesus the author of our peace but because of his perfect blood sacrifice, he has become our intercessor allowing us to have direct communication with God the Father, the Holy Spirit and himself. His purpose, to offer redemption to all souls, is what we see and want to share with others when our eyes are enlightened. Christ's righteousness and the opportunity for us, by grace, to lay claim on eternal life is the only hope for us and for others. Our focus is blurred when we neglect the calling to offer the hope of Christ to the hopeless.

Read Romans 5:21. Meditate on that scripture. Paraphrase what the Lord is speaking to you through it.

Read Romans 2:9-11.

Christ's purpose was to restore righteous relationships with mankind. Those that have an authentic relationship with God are the results of Christ's hope being realized. Attaining that relationship with Jesus and then engaging in Godly relationships are the visible results of his purpose. Relationships that are cultivated because of the sacrifice of Jesus are what he came to obtain and offer. They are the fruit of his labor. They are the riches of his glory.

Read Malachi 3:16-17. Based on this scripture, what word or phrase could you use to describe your value in God's eyes?

Read Hebrews 2:14-18.

If Christ's hope was to provide a way for us to live eternally with him and his riches are the people that choose to follow his way, then the power of God lies within the link that joins the two. This determining factor is the sacrifice of Jesus. His miraculous birth, sinless life and voluntary death provided a spotless blood capable of reconciling all humans to holiness. The claiming of that blood coupled with the resurrection of our Savior and his ascension to heaven allows us to live eternally with him. No greater power exists. When we keep our eyes on Jesus, the life, we don't need to fear death or anything lesser because the power of our God is so great it can't be outdone (John 14:6).

Read John 14:6. Describe the power of Jesus referencing only this scripture.

As wonderful as it is to have our eyes enlightened, it is impossible for us to obtain this through the flesh. We must be the riches of Christ, resting in his power and then we need to pray. Just as wisdom is gained when we ask for it, our eyes will be enlightened too if we make our request known to God. Ephesians 1:17 says that we should ask God to give us the spirit of wisdom and for revelation in the knowledge of Jesus. The result of this prayer will be enlightened eyes. We will be focused on sharing the gospel and glorifying our God. We should ask for this now because blindly walking around the battlefield is hazardous to us and our allies.

"See then that ye walk circumspectly, not as fools, but as wise, Redeeming the time, because the days are evil." Ephesians 5:15-16

Take time to pray for vision that is Christ-focused.

A similar prayer might be: Lord, thank you for valuing me so much that you shed your blood so that I would have the hope of spending eternity with you. Thank you for using me to share your gospel. Jesus, I pray that the spirit of wisdom would descend upon me and that you would give me your knowledge Lord so that I will be focused on you and make wise decisions that glorify you. I am here for you as yours. In the power of your name I pray, Jesus. Amen.

As mentioned above, the precursor to having enlightened eyes is to have the spirit of wisdom and a God-given understanding of the Word. These benefits aren't randomly bestowed upon people. They aren't self-taught. This wisdom and knowledge only derives from a relationship with God. There isn't any other way to acquire them.

Jesus is the greatest example we have to look to for a goal-oriented person. He understood his purpose was to give his life so that we could receive life eternal. Every decision was made with this goal in mind: to provide a sacrifice capable of redeeming lost souls. Christ was all human just as much as he was all God (Hebrews 2:9, John 1:1 and John 1:14). He had to put forth effort to not sin (Hebrews 4:15). He had to put forth effort to be spiritually focused too. He had to seek out the spirit of wisdom and an understanding of the Word. He did this by communing with his father and studying the scriptures.

Communing with The Father

For Christ to keep focused, he relied upon the guidance from his father. Therefore, he made time to meet with him in prayer. Jesus was known to speak with his father before the sun had risen for the day (Mark 1:35). He also ended his days in communion with his father (Mark

6:46-47). He not only met routinely for prayer, but he also spoke to God throughout the day whenever he or those around him needed guidance (Luke 22:41-42 and John 11:41-44).

Jesus didn't walk through his life hoping that The Father would know his undirected thoughts. Prayer wasn't frivolous to him. It didn't happen coincidentally or insincerely. All of Christ's prayers had a common thread: they were intentional and purposeful. He was intentional in that he directed the conversation, always beginning his prayer with "Father". The prayers were purposeful in that they were always made seeking after God's glory. The intention and purpose of Christ's prayers are derivative of Christ's humility. Jesus set his flesh aside and sought only the wisdom that comes from above. This state of mind resulted in the spirit of wisdom descending upon him.

Jesus had several places that he resorted to when speaking with his father. One of those places was the garden of Gethsemane.

Read John 18:1-2.

Jesus spent enough time here that the disciples knew the place as a safe haven for Christ. Jesus taught that we should have a place dedicated to meeting with God (Matthew 6:5-6). Do you have a "prayer closet"? If so, where is that place for you? If not, I encourage you to devote an area as a place you can go to speak with The Father.

Read Matthew 26:36-46.

Christ's prayer in the garden of Gethsemane shows the need Christ had for the spirit of wisdom to descend upon him. Jesus knew that the time had come for him to give himself as a sacrifice for mankind. But in the flesh he needed encouragement to submit to God's will. He directed his prayer "O Father," and then he gave his request "if it be possible, let this cup pass from me:" He continued to devote himself to purposefully pray that God would be the one to receive glory by finishing the prayer with "nevertheless not as I will, but as thou wilt".

Finally he returned to his disciples and said "the hour is at hand, and the Son of man is betrayed into the hands of sinners." Jesus had entered the garden seeking The Father's guidance and left the garden certain of the wisdom that God had bestowed upon him. Jesus left this time of prayer fully submitted to the spirit of God's wisdom.

This intentional, purposeful conversation with God enlightened Christ's eyes. Jesus was reminded of the hope of his purpose, the riches he stood to gain- us, and the great power he possessed as God. This prayer changed the course of eternity for all mankind. We were on the brink of being left without hope until Jesus sought the wisdom of God. Prayer for the spirit of wisdom is that important.

The example of Christ's prayer in the garden is applicable to our prayer lives. Intentionally meet with God, determining to bring him glory. The submission to his wisdom and will is worth whatever sacrifice is required.

Studying the Scriptures

Heavenly wisdom and the Word never contradict. For this reason we can better recognize the wisdom of God through the study of the scriptures.

Luke 4:18-19 records Jesus standing in the synagogue and reading the passage of scripture referenced to Isaiah 61:1-3 "The Spirit of the Lord is upon me, because he hath anointed me to preach the gospel to the poor; he hath sent me to heal the brokenhearted, to preach deliverance to the captives, and recovering of sight to the blind, to set at liberty them that are bruised, to preach the acceptable year of the Lord."

After reading and meditating on that scripture there wasn't any doubt in the mind of Jesus of what was expected of him. After he sat down he said to the people in attendance, "This day is this scripture fulfilled in your ears." (Luke 4:21).

Jesus knew what was expected of him. He had studied the Word. He entered his prayer closet at Gethsemane fully realizing his intended purpose of coming to this world. He was in need of strength from his father to accomplish it. His flesh wasn't eagerly anticipating the idea of being beaten and sentenced to death in spite of his perfectness. But, because of his knowledge of the Word and willingness to follow God's wisdom, He was able to leave the time of prayer assured that the sacrifice he would make would glorify God and offer redemption to the human race.

Prayer to the Father and study of the scriptures were essential to Christ's eyes being enlightened to the hope of his purpose, the riches of his glory and the greatness of the power of God.

Write about an instance in which your knowledge of the scriptures, paired with prayer, guided you into following after God's will for your life.

Christ's example is for our learning. Engage in consistent, intentional, purposeful conversation with God and use the Word as your reference to confirm what you believe the wisdom of the Lord to be. In doing so, your eyes will be enlightened. You will be reminded that mankind is the reason of Christ's coming, that we are the joy that was set before Jesus and it was for our benefit that he was raised from the dead (John 3:16, Hebrews 12:2, Romans 8:11).

Lesson Five: Looking Out for Each Other

James 2:15-16 states "If a brother or sister be naked, and destitute of daily food, And one of you say unto them, Depart in peace, be ye warmed and filled; notwithstanding ye give them not those things which are needful to the body; what doth it profit?"

Ministry goes beyond acknowledging a need. Ministry, because of compassion, attempts to fulfill the need through generously giving. We are to help those in need as we honor God by following after Jesus' example.

Needing the Ministering

Jesus' ministering here on earth was approaching completion as he entered into the garden of Gethsemane on the eve of his crucifixion. His prayer and knowledge of the scripture allowed him to see through enlightened eyes. He knew that his life, death, burial, resurrection and ascension were the display of love that would be used to draw us to him (Hosea 11:4). These acts of love had been, and were continuing to be, demanding of Jesus, both physically and spiritually. Therefore, he allowed people that he had forged relationships with to minister to him. (To truly minister, voluntarily and out of joy, not as a result of prideful command as was referenced in Matthew 20:28 and Mark 10:45.) Jesus, being our ultimate example, gives us the perfect picture of how we should allow ministry to affect our lives through both receiving and giving.

Jesus needing ministered to may sound odd, but remember he was just as much human as he was God. Throughout Jesus' time on earth he relied on different people to take crucial roles in his ministry.

From the beginning of his life on earth Jesus, from time to time, was reliant on humans. A woman had to be willing to carry Christ in the womb. Mary was willing to do this for Christ (Luke 1:26-38). He relied on John to baptize him in the Jordan River (Matthew 3:13-17). The Word records the women that stood at the foot of Jesus' cross as the ones that ministered to Christ in Galilee. Mark 15:40-41 says "There were also women looking on afar off: among whom was Mary Magdalene, and Mary the mother of James the less and of Joses, and Salome; (Who also, when he was in Galilee, followed him, and ministered unto him;) and many other women which came up with him unto Jerusalem." Christ benefited from these ladies' loyalty to follow after him, caring for him and encouraging him as he went about his father's business. In their faithfulness to minister unto him, he was encouraged to continue down the path his father had laid out before him: ministering to others.

Read Mark 1:40-42.

The leprous man wanted to be free of his condition. He was able to go to Christ with his desire because Jesus was available. He also recognized that Jesus possessed what he stood in need of: healing power. The man asked Jesus to minister to him. Jesus responded by having compassion on the man. He acknowledged the leper's desire to be cleansed and that he was capable of doing that for him. Jesus, through his power and authority, generously gave the man the healing he sought after.

In this, Jesus has given us the model for ministering: He made himself available, he allowed himself to be compassionate and he chose to be generous with the gifts that he possessed.

Mary followed after Christ's example in her ministry towards Jesus. She was one of the people that Jesus relied on to minister to him in a time of need. Mary and her siblings are mentioned on different occasions throughout the gospels as those that shared a mutually beneficial relationship with Christ. Jesus often visited them in their home as he traveled through their town (Luke 10:38-42, John 12:1-8). They were around each other often enough that he referred to them as friends (John 11:11). They were known as being loved by Christ (John 11:5). The four carved out time to be available for one another. That time spent together afforded them a level of comfort and trust. This time set aside for fellowship also provided an opportunity for Mary to minister to Jesus' needs.

Read John 12:3-8.

Their availability to one another resulted in a relationship built on God's love. Mary, recognizing who Christ was, was looking to show Jesus reverence by acting compassionately and giving generously. She entered into his presence intending to minister to Jesus with a pound of spikenard concealed in an alabaster box. The ointment wasn't something that she had just happened upon. Not only did it have great monetary value, but it was part of her future security. Yet, she purposefully chose to give up her plans to glorify and honor Christ. She was making every effort to let him know that she was devoted to him and his cause. This thought process is the beginning of ministering for Jesus' glory. We, like Mary, need to be willing to bury our fleshly desires and self-made plans to rise up in the newness of Christ and live for him (Galatians 2:20, II Corinthians 5:17).

Jesus deemed her actions as completion of part of the Jewish burial customs. This ministry he received from her would be forever recorded as welcomed and ordained by him. Christ had been dependent on Mary's obedience to readily serve him compassionately and generously.

How does it make you feel knowing that the Lord of all creation allowed himself to be ministered to?

Jesus, in the flesh, was available to sit down with Mary and accept her ministering. We lack an opportunity to meet face to face with Christ on this side of eternity. But this doesn't necessarily mean that our occasion to minster to him is lost. Instead our ministering to Jesus takes on a different approach.

Ministering to the Needing

Read Matthew 25:34-40.

Jesus mentioned people that required physical needs to be taken care of. He also spoke of people that were struggling emotionally and spiritually. We minister to Christ by reaching these people. Matthew 25:40 records Jesus as saying "…Inasmuch as ye have done it unto one of the least of these my brethren, ye have done it unto me."

It may be difficult for you to minister to someone for a variety of reasons. It could be that it would seem too stressful for you to sacrifice your time. It may be that you lack compassion because you aren't capable of empathizing with those in need. It might be difficult for you to give from your own resources to help someone.

But just because it isn't easy to do doesn't mean it isn't worthy of being done. Jesus took time away from Heaven to come minister to us. He had known no sin but came to earth to die as a result of sin because a perfect sacrifice was needed and only he could fulfill the requirements. He literally gave himself, paying the ultimate price, so that we would have the opportunity to live with him for eternity. As followers of Christ, we should live grateful for his love and ministry toward us. We should be creating opportunities to deepen our relationship with Jesus. We should look to meet with him daily. Our life's goal should be to honor him. Jesus teaches that we can do this, in part, by serving others in his stead.

Since Christ allowed himself to be ministered to it stands to reason that we, being made in his likeness, are in need of being ministered to (Genesis 1:27). But for some of Christ's followers accepting ministry may be difficult because it shows a need for someone else's help. Some may feel that they only deserve to give and aren't worthy of receiving ministry from the hands of man. Others may determine that they are better off without another person's assistance. Regardless of the reason, rejection of ministry is rooted in pride or vanity. I Peter 5:6 teaches us to "Humble yourselves therefore under the mighty hand of God, that he may exalt you in due time:"

Jesus didn't deny Mary's attempt to minister to him. He honored the self-sacrificing devotion that was shown to him through her work. He understood that God the Father was in the midst of the care given unto him. We, like Christ, should take comfort in knowing that God is looking after our needs. We shouldn't push ministering away. We should recognize ministering as part of our Heavenly Father's divine plan coming to fruition through his chosen vessels.

I Peter 4:10 "As every man hath received the gift, even so minister the same one to another, as good stewards of the manifold grace of God." How could you use the gift God has given you to minister to others?

If we look back to the account of the healing of the leper we see that this is a picture of how we can be blessed through the ministry of a fellow Christian. The leper acknowledged that he needed help. He didn't run from Christ's answers; he ran to him. Rather than allowing embarrassment or shame to keep him from the good gift that he knew Christ possessed, this leper chose to humble himself, admitting that he stood in need of what only Jesus could offer. The man knew that he could trust Jesus' work in his life.

Be willing to become a recipient of ministering. Accept what God has for you whether it is given through a teacher, a pastor, a friend, a family member or a random person that you may never meet.

Is there someone that the Lord has called you to receive ministering from? How have you responded to their outpouring of compassion and generosity?

Ministry: Full Circle

We know that Jesus favors both the receiving and giving of ministry. He allowed himself to be ministered to as he ministered to others. Consequently, The Father received glory from Christ's involvement of ministry on earth. Not only did Christ give us a prototype of how to minister and to receive ministry but he showed us who would receive the glory. The words of Christ as he spoke with his father are recorded in John 17:4 "I have glorified thee on earth: I have finished the work which thou gavest me to do." Christians should work together to lift up the name of Jesus. Just as Jesus had a mind frame of continually ministering even as he was being ministered to, we can simultaneously be recipients as well as givers.

Read Acts 10:1-44.

Cornelius sought the Lord frequently. He was devout in bringing God glory. He was given the opportunity to open his doors and to gather an audience to receive a message from the Lord. He was compassionate in deepening his own relationship with God as well as others'. The Lord spoke to him because he was willing. He lacked only the resource, the message, which needed to be given.

Through a vision from the Lord, Peter was being given a message to spread. This message would bring hope to the Gentile people, including Cornelius and those gathered at his house. Peter developed a compassionate desire for seeing the message he had been given proclaimed. He was willing to share it with whomever the Lord chose. He lacked only the opportunity to do so.

God, through an angel, arranged for Peter and Cornelius' paths to intersect. Peter, in an attempt to minister for God accepted the ministry offered to him by Cornelius, orchestrated by God. Cornelius was found in a similar situation as he ministered to God. He had received the gift he had been seeking to gain as a result Peter's ministry. The men offered to God what they had. God utilized their gifts to build his kingdom. The willingness of these two men that were compassionately living for God and were continuingly making themselves available to see his will performed in their lives brought their relationship with Christ, as well as many others, to an entirely new level. Every person in the house full of people was blessed because of God's desire to use his people to minister to one another.

We are the body of Christ. We work most efficiently when we work together. We thrive when we surround ourselves with one another. Our gifts differ. Our goal is the same. The ministry you are part of is being done to glorify him. Ephesians 4:11-12 says "And he gave some, apostles; and some, prophets; and some, evangelists; and some, pastors and teachers; For the perfecting of the saints, for the work of the ministry, for the edifying of the body of Christ:"

Of availability, compassion and generosity, which do you have most difficulty sharing? Which do you have the most difficulty receiving?

Go to prayer asking the Lord to help you to overcome these blocks separating you from being actively involved in ministering.

A similar prayer might look like this: Lord, thank you for your Word. Thank you for showing us through your actions that we are allowed and it is even necessary for us to be ministered to by our family of God. I'm asking you to keep my pride from making decisions for me. I want to be used by you and for you. I know that you have given me opportunities to share my gifts and that there are times when I have been offered ministering from others. Help me to be both a giver and a receiver, just as you were. You know there is nothing more that I'd rather do than to follow the path you have paved yourself. In Jesus' name I pray. Amen.

Lesson Six: The Hero in Us

"Know ye not that ye are the temple of God, and that the Spirit of God dwelleth in you?" I Corinthians 3:16

Without Jesus coming to this earth, living a sinless life, shedding his spotless blood and raising again we would have zero hope of being able to have a relationship with God the Father. Similar to Jesus being the link between us and The Father, we are the connection that is chosen to introduce people to a relationship with Jesus. Jesus has shown us the wisdom in cultivating Christ-honoring relationships: these relationships lead to ministering opportunities and with ministering comes opportunities for intercession.

Read II Corinthians 5:18-21.

From the moment that Jesus chose to leave heaven until the moment in which he returned,

Christ focused on ministering (Hebrews 10:9-10). The wisdom that Christ beheld as he went through life on earth has the potential to affect every part of our walk with him. We have learned to view things in the spiritual realm, to study the scriptures, to pray for guidance. We have studied the importance of a relationship with The Father. Not only has Christ emphasized this through his actions but he also taught us, through example, that ministering, both receiving and giving of it, is helpful and necessary in fulfilling God's work in our life. Jesus' ministry led to intercession on our behalf through his death, resurrection and ascension. The choices Jesus made not only ministered to us but also allowed him the ability to become our mediator (I Timothy 2:5-6). Christ's ministry-mindset provided numerous opportunities for him to intercede for the people he walked the earth with. Today we choose him as our mediator by accepting salvation through his name and also as our intercessor by continuing to trust in him (Romans 5:9, Hebrews 4:14-16).

"Wherefore he is able also to save them to the uttermost that come unto God by him, seeing he ever liveth to make intercession for them." Hebrews 7:25

The ministry of reconciliation experienced first-hand gives us a testimony to relay to others. It follows the model that Christ gave. We die to our sin, live in the newness of Christ and will one day rest for eternity in heaven. Since we have chosen this for ourselves we can participate in ministry that leads to intercession on behalf of others. We take on the role of ambassador in honor of Christ. Our path of redemption becomes a road that others can follow.

Read II Corinthians 3:3.

One way that we are able to act as a go-between for others is to live in obedience to the Spirit of God. Our surrender to the Spirit allows the characteristics of Jesus to be evident in our life. Some people may never be given an opportunity to read the gospel from the pages of the Bible. This doesn't exclude them from obtaining salvation. Instead, they are introduced to the power of Christ by observing people that have chosen Christ, which is us. Our choices, the life we live, become a reflection of Jesus.

Galatians 5:22-23 and Colossians 3:12-15 are two passages of scripture that list traits a Christian should possess. What are they?

Learning what Christians should be known for displaying helps makes us more intentional in following Christ. Of the list given, which comes easiest for you to offer? Which is most difficult for you to act on?

Our actions may be what determine a person's decision to follow or reject Christ. We may never be aware of who we are impacting because we fail to see the potential to make an impression. The fact is every person is required to make a decision; therefore, our readiness and willingness to live according to the Word should be of upmost importance.

Yes, Please.

Read Luke 13:1-5.

In this passage of scripture Jesus reminds us that no person's sin is any more or any less significant than another's sin. Without repentance, coupled with the redeeming quality of Christ's blood, a person stands in need of a savior. Remember, you are free of damnation because Jesus chose to minister to you through his death on the cross and was therefore able to become your mediator. Accepting the ministering of others and the work Christ completed on our behalf begins to resonate within us when we acknowledge that this is why we are no longer lost. Sharing Christ's love with the unsaved may become less daunting and more attainable when we remember that we once stood where the unsaved are standing now and they are on the same path to Hell that we were before Jesus saved us.

Been There, Done That

Saul was renowned for his study and keeping of the Jewish law. Still, he stood as a devout Jew in need of a savior. On the road to Damascus he met Jesus and accepted him as his Lord (Acts 9). After that encounter God changed his name and Saul became known as Paul. Paul had a desire to share the gospel with the people that were standing where he once stood.

Read Acts 18:4-6.

Paul felt compelled to share that Jesus was the Christ with the people that he had once been linked to. These were the people he could empathize with. He spoke in the synagogues, trying to reason with them, using their shared knowledge to validate his point. He knew the life the Jews were living was meaningless because they hadn't received salvation through the Messiah. He felt obligated to share his experience with the people he had previously identified with, in hopes of winning them to Christ.

Sadly, the Jews turned Paul away; ultimately they were rejecting Jesus Christ. They decided not to believe the gospel. The Word teaches us that not everyone will accept Jesus' plan of salvation. To us, this means that we will witness rejection just as Paul did with these Jews. Jesus knew that this would happen. He sent out his disciples in pairs, making them fully aware that they wouldn't be well received in some places but reassuring them that their responsibility was to share the ministry of reconciliation, not to save souls (Mark 6:11). Our duty is to present the gospel; once it is given the individual becomes personally responsible for their decision to accept or reject Christ.

Paul had acted as an ambassador to these people, regardless of their chosen outcome. Paul knew that he would be held accountable based only on his obedience to the Lord, just as the disciples were. Therefore, he could leave the presence of the Jews content that they had been given the same opportunity to accept Christ as their mediator, just as he had been given.

Empathy for the unsaved and obedience to the Lord heavily factor into reaching the unsaved. Your heart may be hardened to sharing the gospel because you lack one of the two. If so, use the space below to speak to the Lord, asking him to soften your heart. It may sound something like this:

Jesus, remind me of the goodness of your blood. The value of your blood being applied to my life is the only reason I have eternity with you. Without it I would still be faced with eternal damnation. Help me to remember that no one needs to earn your blood but that you freely give it. Your blood is capable of cleansing anyone. Help me to share the gospel with those that are in need of hearing it, just as someone did for me. Remind me Lord, that without obedience from your children the gospel will have a hard time being spread. You are using me to be a picture of you, Jesus. Make me to be empathetic to those without you. Help me to be obedient so that you can use me. I am here to bring you glory, to see souls saved and to see you lifted up. In Jesus' name I pray. Amen.

Imitating the Ultimate Intercessor

If we were to oversimplify Christ's work it would look something like this: Jesus' driving force is to honor his father by having a positive impact on people's choice for where they will spend eternity. He is effective because he is relatable to people, takes part in ministry as God leads and has literally given his life in hopes that we will call on him to make intercession on our behalf.

As ambassadors we not only need to be faithful to follow the example Jesus gives, but we also should do our part in executing it. Sacrificing our lives to allow Christ to live in us sounds overwhelming and intimidating. On our own it would be impossible. Therefore, God sent the Comforter to teach us (John 14:26). Within the New Testament there is record of people benefiting from and promoting the work of Jesus by accepting a relationship with The Father, ministering to one another and interceding in people's lives to bring them to Christ. Three men in particular, Philemon, Paul and Onesimus, have a portion of their story written in this part of the Word. The moving of The Spirit was evident in the lives of these men.

Read Philemon 1:1-21.

If we look a little closer to the scriptures we can determine that Paul met Philemon and Onesimus in different chapters of his life. He was a free man when he met Philemon in his hometown, most likely traveling as a missionary ministering to the people as an ambassador for Christ. He kept contact with Philemon, holding him accountable as he matured in the faith. Later we learn that Paul became bound as a prisoner for Christ. In this setting he became the one that stood in need of ministering. Onesimus, after accepting the plan of salvation as Paul had presented it to him, became the one that The Spirit used to minister to Paul.

What do you find most intriguing about Paul's experience with ministry? The fact that God used him regardless of his current situation or that he, being a mature Christian, would be comforted and ministered to by the work of men that he had the pleasure of leading to Christ?

Philemon was a wealthy man. He had servants. He hosted church meetings in his home. He was also well-respected by Paul because of how he represented Christ. Philemon treated his fellow brethren with love, without regard to their social status. Perhaps the enemy (Satan) used this to grate on Philemon's servant, Onesimus' nerves. Regardless of the reason, Onesimus fled from Philemon's home determined that a place graced with God's love wasn't for him. The path that took him far from Philemon led him directly to Paul, the intercessor Christ chose to share the ministry of reconciliation.

As recorded in Luke, God doesn't reserve his blood for only a select few. Just as it was valuable to the servant that was running from his past, it was accepted by the man that was content in the present.

Read II Corinthians 4:18. Have you allowed people's past or present situations to deter you from ministering to them? Why shouldn't a person's temporary state affect our willingness to be effective in their life?

Paul, in his old age, was no longer able to write down letters himself. He relied upon the help of those that he trusted to write for him. Onesimus became a trusted companion of Paul's which led to Onesimus writing Paul's words for him. Interestingly, Paul's letter to Philemon was penned down by Onesimus. Within the letter Paul acts as the intercessor between the two men, vouching for both of their character. Paul plainly stated Onesimus' wrongdoing while simultaneously asking Philemon to go above and beyond what was expected of him and offer grace that Onesimus stood in need of.

The picture that these men's lives portrayed is applicable to every one of us. We were once the runaway servant that God had enough mercy upon to ask his only begotten Son to offer a willing sacrifice as a covering for our sin.

The Word doesn't record if Philemon received Onesimus as a brother like Paul suggested he do. Do you think that Philemon accepted or rejected Onesimus? What is your answer based on? If someone were to determine if you would offer grace, what do you think they would say? What evidence is there to support that?

Paul, Philemon and Onesimus lived in the last days, just as we do today. They had the same Spirit living within them that we have living within us. Their ministries and intercessions were used by God to bring him glory. You are capable of the same work of faith. You are an ambassador for Christ.

Meeting Two: Peaceful Relationships

"And we beseech you, brethren, to know them which labour among you, and are over you in the Lord, and admonish you; And to esteem them very highly in love for their works sake. And be at peace among yourselves." I Thessalonians 5:12-13

Promises of Peace

I am so grateful for the peace that comes along with salvation and wisdom. I have, like everyone else, faced many battles since becoming a follower of Christ. One battle I fought was feeling useless in God's kingdom.

My husband and I had just moved our family hours away from everything we knew. We were in an unfamiliar area. Nobody knew us; therefore, it took a while before people were willing to let us work within their church. I went from teaching every Sunday, Monday and Wednesday to not teaching at all. I was distraught. While sitting in Sunday School class of our new church, the Lord spoke to me. The lesson had been taken from one of Paul's letters that he had penned down while in confinement. The Lord opened my eyes. If Paul could be used while he was in captivity then the Lord could use me to reach people from where I was too. From this revelation my blog, Leaving a Legacy Ministries, was born. I had felt forgotten but realized that the Lord didn't see me that way. I learned that it was Satan trying to convince me that I was of no use anymore. I also realized that the Lord had already given me everything that he was calling me to do. That day a spiritual battle was won that has led me to many opportunities to fulfill the calling God has put on my life.

Share a battle in your life that you, through the wisdom of the Lord, have come out as a conqueror.

Christian Camaraderie

Solomon's father, King David, was able to mentor Solomon as he came up under his guidance. David not only spoke words of wisdom into Solomon's life but he also chose to live wisely, for the most part. As we mature in our faith we should be a people that take part in relationships and in ministering. This shouldn't be taken lightly. Our actions have the potential to reach generations we may never see.

God has entrusted my husband and I with three children to train up in his ways. We, by default, have become their mentors. We have intentionally made efforts to make our home a place that honors Jesus. Scripture is quoted from the rising of the sun to the going down of the same (Psalm 113:3). We try to model what a relationship with Jesus looks like by regularly going to Christ with praise, for guidance and with requests (Psalm 143:10). We are determined, through the grace of God, to make our home a place of forgiveness because Christ forgave us.

You are living an example for people to see, regardless if you are aware of whom you may be impacting. What wisdom are you sharing with others that may be watching you? Share with the group what you hope to convey as a mentor.

Following Your Commander

Authentic relationships require time to be invested and wise decisions to be made. Jesus gave us examples for pursuing a relationship with The Father. Through prayer and study of the scriptures Christ was able to fulfill the purpose for which he came to earth. He was reminded of the hope he had to offer, the riches he stood to gain and the power that he possessed. This models for us the necessity to commune with The Father to be able to diligently seek out his will for our life.

I know that I have been called to be a teacher of the Word. It is the gift that the Lord has given me, along with many other teachers he has called to edify the body of Christ. I prefer to teach in a classroom setting, whether that is Sunday School, Vacation Bible School or youth camps. However, as I have continued to teach, the platform has expanded to blogging which eventually led to a calling to write biblical study guides.

As certain as I was that the Lord called me to teach the Word, I was very hesitant to write a study guide. I prayed for months, seeking a conviction that this is what the Lord was leading me to do. In church on Sunday morning, October 20, 2013, the Lord convinced me that he was again expanding the way he would use me as a teacher. He showed me through his Word that this was his will for me. The scripture that was used to confirm the calling was John 15:16 "Ye have not chosen me, but I have chosen you, and ordained you, that ye should go and bring forth fruit, and that your fruit should remain: that whatsoever ye shall ask of the Father in my name, he may give it you." This is one of my very favorite verses because it is a vivid reminder that the Lord communicates with me and that he has a purpose for my life.

Scripture is reassuring and concrete. It is a lamp unto our feet and a light unto our path (Psalm 119:105). Share with the group one of your favorite pieces of scripture and why or how the Lord has spoken to you through it.

Looking Out for Each Other

Jesus was the most influential minister to ever walk this earth. He knew what people stood in need of. He, being God, was completely aware of and focused on impacting the hearts of his creation. He knew that each person would have to make a decision for their eternity. Each encounter he had with people revolved around this: glorifying God so that others would come to choose to live for him. From some of these opportunities, real relationships formed between Christ and the needy.

Being as I am one of the needy, I can say that I am so grateful that he chose to minister to me. Not only has his life, death, and resurrection been monumental in my life but the day to day interaction with him causes me to feel strengthened and capable of moving forward.

I look forward to the Lord ministering to me through the preaching of his Word on Sundays. I am amazed at how he affirms, corrects and encourages me through another one of his servants. The ministry I receive on a weekly basis strengthens me in my weakness. Miraculously, because of the Holy Spirit, the same messages that affect me so greatly are impacting an entire congregation that is seeking the Lord's will for their life. I am so grateful when God's children are obedient in using their gift to minister to others. God is glorified and the church is edified.

The Lord is looking out for those that love him (Romans 8:28). He is evident in your daily life. How so? Share with the group how the Lord has ministered to you lately.

The Hero in Us

A great honor is bestowed upon us when we accept Jesus as our savior. Not only are we granted salvation but we also gain the privilege of being used by Christ to reach our neighbors. Even more amazing than that is the truth that we must only be willing and obedient. He directs our steps to where we should go. He fills our mouths with the words to say. We benefit from the work that Christ does in us, around us and through us.

"Not that we are sufficient of ourselves to think any thing as of ourselves; but our sufficiency is of God;" II Corinthians 3:5

The month that my oldest child turned four, my husband and I moved our young family a day's trip from everything we had ever known. We were certain that we were following the Lord's will for our lives. Naturally our children would miss their family members and would ask to move back to our old house. Shortly after we moved, I specifically remember my daughter approaching me with her desire to move back. I was heartbroken that she was so sad. I prayed, asking the Lord to use me to help her in this difficult time. Immediately the story of the prodigal son came to my mind. I retold the story to her as she watched me wide-eyed and listened intently. She then understood, on her level, that being in the Lord's will was the only place a person could find peace. Since then she has been content to live where we are living. She is a happy child and I am so grateful that the Lord used me to share peace with her.

One of the most rewarding experiences as a follower of Christ is to recognize that you have been used as an ambassador by God to help someone in need. Share an experience with the group that you have been blessed to be part of.

From birth to death, we are involved in relationships. The way in which we choose to manage our relationships is indicative of where we obtain our wisdom. Graciously as always, Christ has given us the perfect model to follow. Learn from the mentors he has placed in your life. Reach out to those around you in ministry and, above all else, be the ambassador that Christ has ordained you to be. Relationships are constants in our daily life; interacting in the same manner as Christ did is wisdom that has been obtained from above. In Chapter Three: Victory in Sight, we will be studying the power we possess over the enemy when we remain focused on the battle.

Victory in Sight

"Through thee will we push down our enemies: through thy name will we tread them under that rise up against us." Psalm 44:5

Lesson Seven: Set Up for Victory

In Lesson Two: Promises of Peace, we learned that David's wisdom caused him to obtain peace that passed all understanding. However, this didn't mean that every relationship he had was peaceful. Saul's jealousy of David caused contention between the two men. Saul had once appreciated what David had done for the country. That is until David began receiving more praise than Saul did. Saul, the very same king that had previously chosen to benefit from David's wisdom and relationship with God, now hated him for it. David wasn't responsible for Saul's strife. Saul's pride was. But Saul had misidentified the problem because he chose not to seek the Lord's wisdom. He, having bitter envying within his heart, began making decisions based on devilish, worldly wisdom. His solution to dealing with his pride was to annihilate David with a javelin.

So often we are tempted to take matters into our own hands instead of to the Lord. Write about a time when you chose to deny your way of doing things and chose to rely on the Lord instead.

As children of God we will win every spiritual battle if we cling to the wisdom of God's Word. However, in the physical world there are times in which the devilish wisdom seemingly prevails. If, for example, Saul was able to slay David, the world would say Saul's wisdom won.

This conclusion is misleading because eternity hasn't been factored in. Death is just sleep to a Christian (John 11:11-14). David's loss of life wouldn't have caused him to lose the peace of God and wisdom that he had already attained.

Write about a time when you could rest in the peace of God even though the onlookers from the world thought you had failed.

In this instance David prevailed both in the flesh and spiritually speaking. Saul began to fear David. Twice he had seen him escape death at his own hand. Battle after battle he watched David come back unscathed. No matter what David came up against, Saul watched him stand unharmed. Saul viewed David as a person that was indestructible because he knew that David's protection was from God.

We too can leave a spiritual battle without being wounded or defeated. We can fight through every single conflict and be victorious because of Jesus. He knows what we face. He knows how to lead us to victory.

The Enemy Fears the Wise

Read Matthew 7:24-27.

In this passage Jesus uses a parable to teach the importance of a foundation. Once again the options given are complete opposites. Rock and sand are the only available choices. We, as soldiers of "the good" have chosen to build upon the Rock, Jesus Christ. Notice that our foundation doesn't exempt us from facing storms. It is, however, the anchor that allows us to withstand them.

Our foundation has been laid. Now we must build upon it. In Proverbs 9 the blueprint of a house built by wisdom, personified as a woman, is given. There are seven pillars that are spoken of within this chapter.

Read Proverbs 9.

Pillar One: Being Prepared

"She hath killed her beasts; she hath mingled her wine; she hath also furnished her table." Proverbs 9:2

This woman had food and drinks sitting on the table. She was ready to feed anyone that she could get to come over for dinner. She wasn't going to be caught off guard. Neither should we.

"Study to shew thyself approved unto God, a workman that needeth not to be ashamed, rightly dividing the word of truth." II Timothy 2:15

Stephen lived a life completely surrendered to Jesus. He was so effective in sharing Christ's gospel that the Jewish people hated him. Stephen was arrested because his message went against Jewish custom. As he stood before the Jewish council they gave him opportunity to speak for himself.

Stephen accurately recounted the Jewish history, beginning with call of Abraham and ending at their present day. He knew the scriptures well enough that even the council couldn't dispute what he was saying. He concluded his answer to the council by letting them know that they had murdered the Just One, Jesus Christ (Acts 6:8-7:53).

Stephen could stand before these men and his God as an unashamed ambassador of the gospel because he was prepared to give the truth. Prayerfully study scripture. Know what your convictions are rooted in. Be ready to share why you believe the way you do because "being prepared" is a pillar in the house built by wisdom.

Write down what you would say if you were asked why you follow Jesus.

Pillar Two: Compassion

"She hath sent forth her maidens: she crieth upon the highest places of the city, Whoso is simple, let him turn in hither: as for him that wanteth understanding, she saith to him, Come, eat of my bread, and drink of the wine which I have mingled." Proverbs 9:3-5

Not only is this lady prepared to serve guests but she is actively trying to get them to come have dinner with her. She is offering to feed those that are hungry. She has compassion towards those that are without.

"My little children, let us not love in word, neither in tongue; but in deed and in truth." I John 3:18

Prisoners and prisoner guards had been shipwrecked at sea. They saw the island Melita within swimming distance. Some swam to the land, others floated on pieces of broken ship. Once they finally made it ashore they were cold and wet. The people of Melita recognized the foreigners' situation. Instead of ignoring them or adding to their hardship, they chose to build a fire so they could be warmed. The Melitians chose to have compassion on the other men (Acts 27:39-44 and 28:1-2).

We have opportunities all around us to bless others by acting compassionately. It could be as simple as opening a door for a person that has their hands full or as involved as adopting an orphan into your family. Both situations are examples of purposefully caring for others and both symbolize another pillar in the house built by wisdom which represents "compassion".

Write about a time you were blessed because someone backed up their words with actions.

Pillar Three: Consistency

"Forsake the foolish, and live; and go in the way of understanding." Proverbs 9:6

The woman is consistent in her message. She is telling them again that what she has to offer is what they need for a better way of life. She is standing by her statement that foolish ways need to be forsaken.

"Let not sin therefore reign in your mortal body, that ye should obey it in the lusts thereof." Romans 6:12

The angel of the Lord had spoken with urgency when he told Lot and his family to "escape for thy life". In that moment, Lot understood that the ties from the former life needed to be severed to survive the new one. He realized that one look back wouldn't be worth the risk. His wife didn't grasp the need for such restraint. Lot's wife became a pillar of salt (Genesis 19:15-29).

The temptation to allow ungodly parts of our former way of life to creep into our new one is a battle many fight. Instead of conjuring a plan to try appeasing the flesh, determine to not allow sin to have any ownership in your life. Be consistent in only allowing the Spirit to guide your decisions. Judge your thought process on the Word, not your desires.

What is something that you do that shows that you have resolved to grow in Christ?

Pillar Four: Sensitivity

"He that reproveth a scorner getteth to himself shame: and he that rebuketh a wicked man getteth himself a blot. Reprove not a scorner, lest he hate thee: rebuke a wise man, and he will love thee. Give instruction to a wise man, and he will be yet wiser: teach a just man, and he will increase in learning." Proverbs 9:7-9

The woman lets the passersby know that she will only be serving the people that are willing to come to her. She realizes the backlash of pushing something on someone that doesn't want it. She knows that forcing what she has on others will only harm her reputation.

"For as many as are led by the Spirit of God, they are the sons of God." Romans 8:14

Apollos originally was a disciple of Jesus' forerunner, John the Baptist. Therefore, he knew the scriptures well. He spoke eloquently John's message of outwardly professing the intent to change your life for the better. Apollos didn't despise Christ's message, he just hadn't had the opportunity yet to accept or reject Jesus. Aquila and Priscila, followers of Jesus, being led by the Spirit, taught him about Jesus. Apollos responded by believing in grace. He then became a student of Jesus that traveled the world preaching salvation through Christ in addition to baptism (Acts 18:24-28).

The guiding of the Spirit needs to be present for people to change. Our passion, no matter how intense, isn't capable of transforming a person. The Spirit of God will direct us to the people that he has prepared to hear the gospel of Jesus. We need to be tuned to follow after it. What ways are you assured that the Lord is speaking to you?

Pillar Five: Personal Responsibility

"The fear of the Lord is the beginning of wisdom: and the knowledge of the holy is understanding. For by me thy days shall be multiplied, and the years of thy life shall be increased. If thou be wise, thou shalt be wise for thyself: but if thou scornest, thou alone shalt bear it." Proverbs 9:10-12

The woman has prepared a table, she has opened her doors for people to come and eat. She has offered anyone and everyone to come and partake of her goodness. Now she is putting the responsibility on them. She tells them that their end result will be based upon the choice that they make.

"And if it seem evil unto you to serve the Lord, choose you this day whom ye will serve; whether the gods which your fathers served that were on the other side of the flood, or the gods of the Amorites, in whose land ye dwell: but as for me and my house, we will serve the Lord." Joshua 24:15

Paul stood before the people of Athens and declared unto them the resurrection of Jesus. Some people laughed at him. Other people said that they wanted to know a bit more before they made their decision. But for Dionysus, Damaris and some others this was the day that they chose to believe on Jesus for salvation (Acts 17:22-34).

A person stands alone when they stand before Christ. The only way we will be able to spend eternity with Jesus is if we have accepted his blood as sacrifice for our sin. His sacrifice, like wisdom, isn't just for a select few. It is offered to everyone and anyone willing to accept it. Each person must make their own choice.

Pillar Six: Realistic

"A foolish woman is clamorous: she is simple, and knoweth nothing. For she sitteth at the door of her house, on a seat in the high places of the city, to call passengers who go right on their ways: Whoso is simple, let him turn in hither: and as for him that wanteth understanding, she saith unto him," Proverbs 9:13-16

The lady that has prepared a table for anyone to benefit from acknowledges that she has an imitator. This imitator doesn't want to help others. She wants only to harm them.

"Having a form of godliness, but denying the power thereof: from such turn away." II Timothy 3:5

The Lord had spoken very detailed instructions to the man of God. He was told not to eat or to drink but to head home. The king offered him food and water. The man said no. Then an old man, claiming to be a prophet, persuaded him to go directly against the word of the Lord. He convinced the man of God that he too had heard from the Lord and that it was okay to eat and drink at his house. The man of God believed the lie and paid for his disobedience with his life (I Kings 13:7-24).

The old prophet seemed to have godliness about him. He had a title. He had a reputation. He had a believable story. But he went against the word of the Lord. There are people that will try to pull you down. Not everyone has the Spirit of God within them. If we are to be a wise people then we need to be a realistic people too.

Pillar Seven: Considers the Future

"Stolen waters are sweet, and bread eaten in secret is pleasant. But he knoweth not that the dead are there; and that her guests are in the depths of hell." Proverbs 9:17-18

The woman is telling us that her imitator will make living in sin appealing. She goes on to say that the imposter won't mention that the end of the unwise is an eternity spent in Hell.

"Jesus saith unto him, I am the way, the truth, and the life: no man cometh unto the Father, but by me." John 14:6

Elymas determined to not allow Paul and Barnabas to meet with the deputy. He was adamant about blocking their path because he realized that the deputy's conversion wouldn't be good for his position as sorcerer. Paul understood this man's intentions. Through the power of the Lord, Paul caused Elymas to go blind. Ironically this was what caused the deputy to believe (Acts 13:4-12).

Elymas thought that he was better off trying to make it on his own rather than to be a follower of Christ. His way of thinking was a result of only considering the present time, not the future. An absence of wisdom leads to this mindset. If you are trying to weigh out the options of a major decision I encourage you to consider the future.

List the seven pillars of wisdom.

Read I Samuel 18:15. How did David conduct himself? What was the result of that?

David chose to do the best that he could in the situations that God put him in. He fought when he was sent to fight. It was evident that David was choosing to build upon the firm foundation that he had been set on.

Saul recognized the solid foundation that David had built upon was the source of his strength. This caused Saul to fear David. Wisdom of the Lord causes Satan to fear us. He fears wise warriors because he realizes that people battling with the Lord's wisdom leaves no chance for destruction.

Lesson Eight: Seeing the Field

"But seek ye first the kingdom of God, and his righteousness; and all these things shall be added unto you." Matthew 6:33

In today's lesson we will be going to the Old Testament to study the wisdom of Uzziah. Uzziah was made king over Judah at a young age and resided in Jerusalem during his five decades of rule. He was best known for his war-time strategies. There is one piece of scripture in particular that this lesson is built on. II Chronicles 26:5 "And he sought God in the days of Zechariah, who had understanding in the visions of God: and as long as he sought the Lord, God made him to prosper."

Positioned to Win

Read II Chronicles 26:1-15.

Amaziah, King of Judah, had been assassinated by his own people. The heir to the throne was Uzziah, his sixteen year old son. The circumstances thrust Uzziah into a position of authority without any time for preparation or any personal experiences to learn from. Uzziah handled his newfound responsibility in the best way possible: he turned to God for wisdom. The wisdom that the Lord offered Uzziah, via Zechariah, would prove beneficial. God's counsel always positioned Judah to win. Three principles in particular were crucial to Uzziah's governing: he understood the importance of barriers, the value of land and the benefits of preparation.

Uzziah realized that his responsibility as king was to protect the people of the land. In some instances this meant that his army would have to seek out the enemy. At other times it meant that his men would need to focus on gaining ground. All of the time though, Uzziah had to be anticipating his next move so that an upcoming battle wouldn't overtake his country.

Noted in this passage of scripture are the battles of Gath, Jabneh and Ashdod. These were cities that neighbored Judah and were inhabited by the Philistines. God helped Uzziah to win these battles and to also be victorious over the Arabians. Victory after victory caused people to both admire and fear Uzziah's army.

Daily we have opportunities to strengthen ourselves in the Lord. What is something that you do in your life that causes God to be pleased and consequently gives Satan reason to fear?

Uzziah didn't underestimate the impact of a barrier. After he warred with his enemies he broke down their walls. This is significant because it kept the possibility of the enemy's rebuild exposed. As long as there weren't any walls obstructing Uzziah's view, he knew exactly what he faced.

Similar to an enemy's wall blocking the opponent's view, temptation skews our vision. Imagine lust as the tool that prepares the ground for a structure to be built and temptation as the wall that is built upon it. This creates a perfect barrier put into place for sin to rise up, which results in death (James 1:14-15). Temptation is a tactic of our enemy that deserves immediate response before it leads to destruction. It is meant to interfere with our focus on God.

We can combat temptation before it even begins to take root. Jesus demonstrates an effective way to keep the enemy's walls from being built: through prayer. Write out Matthew 6:13.

Tearing down enemies' walls was as important to Uzziah as building walls of protection on the home front. Putting a partition between his country and the enemy afforded him not only an initial line of defense but also a vantage point from which to see the enemy coming. Uzziah's walls had built-in towers for watchmen to keep guard. Their high position gave them visibility for a far greater distance than keeping watch on the ground would have given. From their stance, the watchmen were able to alert the people of a potential attack. The wall was crucial for the people it was meant to protect.

Given that we are in a battle, it is comforting to know that God serves as a wall of fire round about us (Zechariah 2:5). He offers us defense and protection. Knowing that Jesus is standing guard for us should supply us with the upmost peace. The wall, in the form of his Spirit offers us warning when the enemy is near, alerting us to fight (II Peter 2:9).

But just as much as the wall represents defense, it also embodies offense. Fire is able to expand without ever losing its presence. As long as it is given fuel it flourishes, creating space for additional growth. This is a picture of our walk with Christ. He surrounds us as a wall of fire to protect us, but to also show us that he is willing to allow us to grow if we want to put in the effort to do so. Christ is able to do more through us than we could ever imagine if we are doing it for his glory (Ephesians 3:20-21).

Take time to ask the Lord to show you if there is something he has called you to that you have given up on simply because you weren't sure that he would bless it. Ask for a renewed vision for what you have put away.

Not only did Uzziah know the benefits of keeping enemies' barriers at bay and the wall of protection intact, but he also understood the value of land. After he tore down walls, he didn't leave the land in ruin. Instead, he built cities in the places of what had once been the enemy's territory.

Places in our life that had once been primed to be marked with temptations need to be filled with the things of the Lord. We shouldn't allow recovered areas of our life to stay open for an enemy attack. We need to be actively seeking God's direction, not sitting idly by. Like Uzziah, we need to put life into what had once been a place of death.

Uzziah didn't only focus on problem areas. He also gave attention to making the good land fruitful. In the desert he dug wells that would support his cattle. He had vineyards in the mountains. He used what the Lord had blessed him with to its fullest potential. He prepared himself and his people for success.

We should actively put forth effort into walking closer with God. We can do this by meditating on spiritual songs, memorizing scripture and following the example the Lord has given us (Ephesians 5:19, Psalm 119:16, Matthew 4:19). To be able to see your growth in the Lord, I recommend that you keep records or goals to measure your progress over time. In the space below write down a scripture you'd like to memorize, a song that is meaningful to you or an attribute of Christ that you need to work on.

This brings about the third principle that helped Judah to gain such fame: Uzziah planned to win. He was prepared for potential attacks. Uzziah didn't cower and hide from the enemy; he prepared to face them. This was demonstrated by Uzziah in the way he provided for his army. They had the best weapons and armor. They had catapults from the towers that stood on the wall. Uzziah knew that being caught off guard or unprepared would mean certain death to his people. He was proactive in seeing those odds significantly reduced.

Zoned In

Read II Chronicles 26:16-21.

Uzziah had become ruler of Judah at the age of sixteen. Some of the phrases used to describe the earlier years of his reign were "he did that which was right in the sight of the Lord", "And God helped him" and "he was marvelously helped". At the end of his reign, in which Uzziah was the age of sixty-eight, the rhetoric changed drastically. Instead of favor, we read "his heart was lifted up to destruction", "he transgressed against the Lord" and "he was cut off from the house of the Lord."

Verse five gives the only explanation needed for this type of turnaround: "and as long as he sought the Lord, God made him to prosper." Uzziah's desire for God's wisdom that had been prevalent in his earlier days diminished as he made decisions in his later years. The concept of wisdom being something a person gains because of age is deceptive. Look back to Psalm 111:10 "The fear of the Lord is the beginning of wisdom: a good understanding have all they that do his commandments: his praise endureth forever." Aged people can be wise, but only if they fear the Lord and keep his commandments. Young people can be wise too. They have the same requisite as the old. Wisdom is less about age and more about your active desire for God's presence in your life.

Read Mark 12:41-44.

On this particular day at the treasury we are shown, by Christ, the generosity of the people. Their offerings were reflective of the credit they gave God for the gifts he had bestowed upon them. The poor widowed woman willingly gave her gift back to the Lord. Even though the woman was only able to give a small amount it showed the gratitude, trust and honor that filled her heart for the Lord. Her act said "Here, God. I give it all to you because you gave it to me. You are my only hope for a better future so I put what you have blessed me with in your hands." The rich people held back from the Lord what he had given them. In their reluctance to let go they were claiming ownership of the money, as well as preference of God's gift over honoring God. By only giving out of their abundance, they were saying "I had more of a hand in gaining this than you did, God. I've done well so far. I can handle this by myself."

Perhaps the ages of the people at the treasury weren't mentioned because they weren't influential in their decisions. Instead of their ages determining their wisdom, what they zoned in on was indicative of their desire for God's presence in their life. The widowed woman's focus on God kept the spotlight off of the gift. The rich people's focus on the gift caused them to not be focused on honoring God. We distance ourselves from the Lord when we allow his blessings to blur the lines of who deserves top priority. This can happen at any given time in our life.

We should regularly evaluate the priorities of our life to make sure that they are in the correct order. List the major responsibilities you have. Ask the Lord to show you the way you have them prioritized in your life. If you need to make changes, now is the time to start.

Uzziah had understood from a young age that to honor and trust the Lord was to seek him and follow the ordinances that he had put into place. Day after day he sought the Lord. Each time God was found faithful to Uzziah. Verse sixteen tells us that Uzziah's downfall began when his focus shifted from seeking the Lord to admiring the things that had been given by him. His desire to seek God vanished as he became satisfied in the life he had already attained. Uzziah chose to blind himself to the source of his past blessings, and consequently, the need for God's wisdom in his future. Sadly, Uzziah's previous days had become a distraction for the day he was living in. In his last year of reign, Uzziah chose to ignore the law that permitted only the priests of the tribe of Levi to burn incense unto the Lord. He attempted to enter the sanctuary and present the ritual that he didn't have the liberty to perform. As a result, he became a leper and the kingdom was turned over to Jotham, his son.

Whether you are on day five thousand, eight hundred and forty or twenty-four thousand, seven hundred and ten you should be actively seeking the wisdom of the Lord in your life. We need to be constantly reminding ourselves to focus on our God, not God's gifts or lack thereof. The sure way we will be battle ready, whether we are young or old, is if we are zoned in on obtaining wisdom from our Father.

We have indicators in our routines to evaluate our focus on the Lord. For the people that gave at the treasury, their indicator was their willingness to part with their money. For Uzziah, it was nixing his habit of going to God for wisdom. Make a list of what your routine looks like when you feel as though you are walking closely to the Lord. Maybe it's that you have Christian radio playing in the background or that you make time to regularly meet with Godly influences. Be specific so that you have something to reference when you encounter a time that you need to regroup.

No matter what our age, keeping our line of sight free from obstructions helps us as we evaluate the battle we are facing and the aftermath that follows. In the next lesson we will study Christ's wisdom from a young age and an intense battle that Jesus fought.

Lesson Nine: Perfect Prototype

"The beginning of the gospel of Jesus Christ, the Son of God;" Mark 1:1

Jesus' birth lit up the sky. He was dedicated in the temple, grew in wisdom, was baptized and endured temptation. All of these significant events in the life of Christ took place before he performed his first miracle. During this time frame people didn't always see Christ for who he was. Satan attacked him. Jesus battled. In this lesson we will be studying a couple of occasions that can help us to gain the wisdom of Christ.

Accept the Position God Has Given You

Until Jesus reaches twelve years of age, the only specifics we are given about Christ is that he grew strong in spirit and was filled with wisdom with the grace of God upon him (Luke 2:40). Otherwise, we don't read anything about him except for his birth and his family's travels. However, the information that is recorded of Jesus' childhood can still be influential to us. In the singular recorded account of his pre-teen years, the wisdom Jesus displayed is evident. At a young age the adolescent Christ acknowledged who he was in the family of God.

Read Luke 2:41-52.

Mary pondered several phrases concerning her son, Jesus. The angel told her he'd be called Son of God and the Son of the Highest (Luke 1:32 and 35). The shepherds told her he was Christ the Lord (Luke 2:11). Simeon, a devout man, presented him to the Lord in the temple claiming that he would be a light to lighten the Gentiles and the glory of the Israelite people (Luke 2:32). Still yet, there is record of at least two incidents in the Word where she and other family members made the mistake of trying to undermine Christ's identity because of their earthly connections. One occurrence took place when she and his brothers asked him to leave a group of people that he was ministering to because they wanted to speak to him (Luke 8:19-21, Matthew 12:46-50 and Mark 3:31-35). The first account of a misstep is recorded when she and Joseph reprimanded Jesus for the sorrow they felt because they didn't know his whereabouts.

Not knowing where Jesus was or of his safety would have caused great distress for the parents, as it would most anyone that lost a child in their care. What if he had been captured? What if he had been hurt? What if he was scared? Questions probably raced through their minds. Their emotions probably ran from sadness to anger. When they found him in the temple after three days of frantically searching for him, their initial response was amazement.

Relief that their son was well and whole was quickly followed by interrogation. Respecting him as the "Son of God" wasn't Mary's top priority. She addressed Jesus as "Son" and she referred to Joseph as "thy father". Acknowledging only their earthly roles was telling of her state of mind. She was viewing Jesus just as the world did: as her and Joseph's son. Nowhere in her line of thinking were the thoughts "This is the Son of God. He is doing what is best. This is where his heavenly Father has called him to be." The three of them left the temple together but they weren't seeing eye to eye. Mary and Joseph did not understand what Jesus meant by his statement.

At the initial sign of stress we tend to disregard the spiritual realm. Often, if only briefly, we view the situation only through what we can see with our physical eyes. It is important for us to have hidden scripture in our heart so that we can quickly and effectively realign our focus. I like to use "Wait on the Lord: be of good courage, and he shall strengthen thine heart: wait, I say, on the Lord." Psalm 27:14. Write out scripture that can help you in times of sudden stress.

Their ignorance of Christ's purpose, regardless of if they are to be held accountable for their misperception, burdened their family. In at least this instance, we see where it caused needless stress on themselves and those around them. It is beneficial for us to be able to recognize a person's identity in Christ.

Read Matthew 7:15-20.

Just as important as it is for us to be able to recognize our spiritual brethren, it is equally important for us to be able to identify those that aren't working for God's glory. In this passage of scripture Jesus teaches the importance of knowing who you are learning from by judging the fruit they bear. The purpose of analyzing a person's work isn't to condemn an individual; it is meant to keep us from harm. Some stress that we endure is self induced because we aren't willing to see people for who they are. Wisdom is accepting that not everyone's intentions are God-glorifying and then being able to differentiate between the two types of people.

Ephesians 5:6-7 gives us a warning, but we don't need to fear because we have the fact-checker, the Word, at our fingertips. What are we to be cautious of?

Words are impactful. The Word teaches that there is life and death in the tongue (Proverbs 18:21). The tone in which they are delivered is important too (Proverbs 15:1). The conversation between Mary and Jesus in which she referred to Jesus only as Joseph's son could have planted a seed of doubt in Christ's mind. Her misspoken words could have caused Jesus to become doubtful of whom he was, Christ the Lord. Her lack of comprehension could have caused him discouragement because she didn't recognize the purpose of his life.

But Jesus didn't allow her perception of him to influence his identity or his intentions. Jesus responded to Mary's questioning by stating his purpose for life: to be about his Father's business. This lone statement recorded from Jesus' childhood is wrapped in wisdom that we can learn from.

His answer was twofold in that it addressed how he felt about others' opinions and the way in which he viewed himself. Since Christ wasn't willing to deny himself of the purpose God the Father had given him, he was choosing to not submit to the world's impression of him. Jesus understood that who he was and his calling to provide salvation to the world didn't need to be validated by anyone. Instead of allowing the ignorant words spoken to silence the reason for staying behind, he chose to proclaim it. With those few words he was able to deny all flesh, including himself while honoring God's purpose for his life. Wisdom is seeing people, even yourself, as your Father sees them.

Have you been denying yourself of a calling because you haven't received man's approval? In the space below write down a specific calling on your life. Have you pursued it? If so, thank you for your obedience. Keep seeking to do his will above all others. If you are hesitant to move forward with the calling, ask the Lord to open your eyes to what he would have you to do, regardless of your or other's opinions.

Fight the Battle You Are In

Fast forward approximately two decades to the baptism of Jesus. After he rises up out of the water, the heavens part and the Spirit of God descends upon him. It is at this time that God, speaking with a voice that descended from heaven, confirms what Jesus had said all of those years ago in the temple. The Father says "Thou art my beloved Son, in whom I am well pleased." (Mark 1:9-11).

Read Luke 4:1-13.

Immediately after his baptism Jesus was led into the wilderness by the Spirit. The purpose of this solitude was for Christ to be tempted by the devil (Matthew 4:1). The very thing Satan challenged Christ with was exactly what God had just proclaimed about Jesus: his identity.

Satan began two of the three statements with "If thou be the Son of God". The three propositions were similar in that they required Jesus to value his time on earth more worthy than he did his place in eternity. Caving to the taunts would have given results that wouldn't have been sinful had they been obtained through honorable means. But in these scenarios, the cost in which they would have been acquired would have been detrimental to Christ's purpose for coming to earth. For Jesus to make the food, receive the miracle and gain the power he would have to choose satisfying his flesh momentarily as opposed to providing a spotless sacrifice for man's eternity.

Jesus chose to resist all temptations through the power of the Word. For each statement Satan made, Christ had scripture to speak back to him. Notice Jesus didn't engage in conversation with Satan and he didn't offer his own explanation of why he wouldn't submit to him. But he didn't ignore him either. Instead, he faced the battle head on by using scripture to silence him. Without the power of the Word the enemy would continue to fight, but with the Word the enemy was defeated. Jesus knew that the source for an abundant life lay in the scriptures. Each time the Word was spoken, life was breathed into the situation that was meant to kill and destroy.

Read Ephesians 6:10-17. What is the only weapon mentioned?

To respond to the temptations like Jesus did we need to learn our weapon. Speaking the Word is dually beneficial. It causes us to hear the truth and then to act wisely by choosing the spiritual over the natural. It also leaves Satan defenseless. The confrontation ends; Satan flees; and we, with Christ, stand victorious.

Jesus knew how to battle. People's opinions didn't affect what he knew to be true. He found his life in the Word. We are always wise to follow the examples of Christ. In the next lesson we will be studying our identity based on the Word.

Lesson Ten: The Battle Fought in Solitude

"And be not conformed to this world: but be ye transformed by the renewing of your mind, that ye may prove what is that good, and acceptable, and perfect, will of God." Romans 12:2

Jesus was confident in who he was: God's only begotten Son (John 3:16). People's misconceptions or opinions didn't cause him to doubt or deny his identity. Even in the midst of persecution and death threats Jesus stood firm, boldly claiming his connection to God the Father (John 5:14-18). If our Savior had his identity challenged or scoffed at, then we should be prepared to face this same type of battle. As studied in the last lesson, Christ referenced the Word for strength and the ability to overcome. The Word is the place for us to gain the same power and assurance of our role in God's kingdom.

When we stop relying on the Word and start believing our flesh we have set ourselves up for misery. The Word teaches that entangling ourselves with the cares of this life is a war that we, good soldiers, don't need to be engaged in. (II Timothy 2:4). Feeling the need to validate your identity in God's kingdom based upon your own or another person's standard is destructive. God's judgment isn't based upon man's ideas. Even though we know this truth, our enemy will try to get us to believe otherwise.

We tend to be very critical of our work in the Lord. We are tempted to score ourselves based on the results we see rather than looking at our submission to Christ. This is dangerous because, essentially, we begin to rely on man's reactions instead of God's leading.

Is there something in your life that you could reevaluate through God's standards instead of your own?

Red Flag of Warning

As odd as it may sound, sometimes we find ourselves deep into a battle before we realize that we are head to head with the enemy. To keep this from happening we need to be able to quickly recognize who Satan is. Jesus describes him as "a murderer from the beginning" and the "father of lies" (John 8:44). At the first mention of Satan in the Word, we find evidence supporting Christ's description of him. He worked subtly through deceit to bring death.

From the beginning of mankind God has made us to be a people of free will. In the next piece of scripture we are introduced to the first "if, then" statement of the Word. Our decisions are based on what we believe to be true at that moment in time.

Read Genesis 2:16-17.

God had said to Adam that if he ate of the tree of the knowledge of good and evil then he would die. Adam believed what God said to be the truth. As a result, he refrained from eating of the particular tree to avoid death. Because he chose to abide by God's plan he could live leisurely while reigning over the animals of the earth for eternity.

Read Genesis 3.

We know from the previous scripture reading that God intended for Adam and Eve to live forever in the garden. He warned them to stay away from the tree of knowledge so that they could continue to live blissfully knowing only peace, joy and life.

Satan, on the other hand, wanted them to experience fear, shame, sorrow, pain and death. But he didn't mention death and all the consequences disobedience to their God would bring. Instead, he blatantly contradicted God's word and then ended his statement with the same promise God had given to Adam earlier. Satan knew that they would get exactly what the Lord told them they would: knowledge of good and evil. He also knew the price they would have to pay: their lives.

For us to walk according to God's will we cannot regard Satan as one that has any interest in making our end good. He comes only to kill and destroy (John 10:10). He will use any tactic he can to harm you, including lies. I encourage you to not allow any word that goes against God's Word to influence what you know to be true.

Prepare yourself by choosing a scripture to go to and be ready to stand on. Philippians 4:8 and II Corinthians 10:5 are examples of verses that provide protection from you falling prey to the adversary. Write out a verse that you can memorize as a quick go-to defense.

Eve's thought process was based on a lie that caused her to doubt God. The perfect walk that she had with her husband and her Creator was put into question. Instead of seeing the blessings that surrounded her in the garden, she momentarily allowed herself to be blinded to the evidence of God in her life.

Her perception changed when she looked at the tree through the eye of deceit rather than through God's blessings of truth. She focused her eyes on the tainted promise of the fruit that promised a better version of her. In doing so, she became victim to questioning her self-worth. She started thinking along the lines of "I am not good enough as I am" or "There is more out there for me and I need to obtain it". Thoughts similar to "God doesn't want me to be his equal, that's why he has put that fruit off limits" swirled through her head.

Warring with her own stray thoughts caused her to make the fatal mistake of accepting what the deceiver had said as truth.

We can sit here thousands of years later and shake our heads at Eve wondering how she could be so easily duped. But when we step back and look at our own battles that we fight, we can empathize with her. If we aren't attentive, we too will believe lies. If you are having difficulties making a decision, consider what you are accepting as truth. Take time to ask the Lord to show you if you have believed a lie to be true.

White Flag of Surrender

Read Romans 8:5-14.

For us to live according to God's Word we must receive Jesus as our savior and continue to follow the leading of the Spirit of God. Submission to the Spirit is our reassurance that we are living as the children of God should. It is easier said than done because the potential for spiritual warfare to break out could happen at any time. Verses seven and eight teach that our own minds are at enmity with God, unable to please him.

Our carnal minds lead us to think either too highly or too harshly of ourselves. When we view ourselves as God's children because of Jesus' sacrifice then we will understand that we are worthy and needy at the same time, all recipients of grace. Is there an area of your life that you think Jesus doesn't need to be a part of or is there a part that you believe is so bad off that he doesn't desire to go there? If so, use the space below to commit it to God. He wants to bring light into those places of darkness.

Since we know that Satan will try to undermine our identity, just as he tried with Christ and also Eve, we must learn the facts about who God sees when he looks at us. We need to prepare ourselves for the battle fought in solitude.

A magnitude of responsibility is given to us when we accept Christ. The world's perception of God is vastly dependent upon our interactions with others. Because of this we should choose to represent our Father well by being just, merciful and humble (Micah 6:8); by abstaining from following after the appearance of evil (I Thessalonians 5:22); and through our love for the brethren (I John 4:21). However, perceptions tend to vary depending on personality, history, custom, culture, mood, etc. Thankfully our responsibilities don't define us.

"But as many as received him, to them gave he power to become the sons of God, even to them that believe on his name: Which were born, not of blood, nor of the will of the flesh, nor of the will of man, but of God." John 1:12-13

God names us based on the truth that we build our lives upon. The Scriptures teach that when we believe on Jesus' name and receive him, we inherit a title and an identity at that time of spiritual rebirth: child of God. The world may or may not recognize us as God's children, but it should be the driving factor in how we identify ourselves. Part of wisdom is finding your identity in accordance to God's Word.

Our identity is no longer based on who we are, but who we have surrendered ourselves to. Jesus has many names: Truth, The Lord Our Righteousness, Prince of Peace, Author and Finisher of Our Faith, Author of Eternal Salvation, and Word of God are a few (John 14:6, Jeremiah 23:6, Isaiah 9:6, Hebrews 12:2, Hebrews 5:9, Revelation 19:13).

Read Ephesians 6:10-17. Draw and label a soldier according to this passage of scripture.

Jesus allows us to conquer the battle of identity by giving us the best armor available: himself. Everything that he is, he has offered to you. The armor available to us is evidence that he has purposed you to live for him, that he wants the best for you, and that you are worthy of the price he paid (Ephesians 1:11, Jeremiah 29:11, I Peter 3:18). When God looks at us dressed in the armor and carrying the sword he has provided, he sees his child that has been wrapped in a sacrificial love, has been redeemed regardless of their past and one that is capable of winning any battle they face.

In addition to the armor identifying us as a soldier of Jesus Christ, it also can be used as a tool to train us to take our thoughts captive. The truth should be at the core of every decision you act on. If your thought isn't rooted in truth, it doesn't deserve any attention. Jesus' righteousness should dictate your thoughts, not your own version of correctness. If your desires are contradictory to what Jesus taught then you need to dismiss them. Prepare yourself to be able to share God's gospel at anytime. Hypocrisy doesn't sit well with anyone, including Christ. If you intend to preach the gospel then it should match the life you currently live. Regardless of what comes your way, it is vital that you hold on to your faith. It is too valuable to disregard when it conveniences you. Forgetting your salvation story gives way to dismissing the grace that has been bestowed upon you. Make an effort to praise Jesus for the mercy in your life. And finally, learn your weapon. Study the Word for confidence and strength. If you think you can leave your sword on the shelf without any use then you are putting yourself at a great disadvantage.

Is there a piece of armor that you need to readjust or tighten up? If so, use the space below to write out a plan as you move forward.

Eve made the mistake of identifying herself based on deceit from Satan. This one lie spiraled out of control, causing her to doubt God. The battle lost resulted in death for her and all of mankind. The provision of Jesus' unfailing armor given to us out of God's love reminds us that we never need to question our purpose, our worth or God's plan for us. We can stand victorious in Jesus knowing that we are a child of his.

Lesson Eleven: Benchmark for Success

"He that walketh with wise men shall be wise: but a companion of fools shall be destroyed." Proverbs 13:20

Look at Me

God can create opportunities for intercession in the least of likely places. He can reroute our mission at any given time. When the time comes for making a decision, it is always best to follow God's direction instead of our plans. We may never know whose eternity is dependent upon our choice but we can always be assured that God has a victory in the works.

Read Acts 16:6-15.

Paul and the other missionaries had previously been preaching in Phrygia and Galatia. From there they were forbidden by the Spirit to preach in Asia. They were told to change course and travel to Macedonia. Paul and the men traveled to Philippi, a city in Macedonia, intent on sharing the gospel. On the Sabbath day they planned to seclude themselves for prayer on the banks of the river. Instead, they crossed paths with a group of women with whom they were able to share the plan of salvation. God had opened the heart of a certain lady, Lydia, and she accepted Jesus as her savior.

Imagine if Paul and the others would have continued with their plan in evangelizing throughout Asia. They would have missed their opportunity to share the gospel with Lydia, the lady that was ready to hear about and apply the redeeming blood of Jesus to her life.

The Spirit knows whom to lead us to. Based on our previous studies we see where these three groups of people: the people that weren't ready to hear the gospel message, the ambassadors, and the women at the river, would have been impacted differently had the missionaries followed their plans rather than the leading of the Spirit. How so? (Reference Lesson Three: The Enemy Fears the Wise, A House Built By Wisdom)

Lydia is textbook for a person growing in wisdom. She didn't hide her conversion. Immediately she became an ambassador to her household. Her intercession for these people gave opportunity for them to accept Jesus' sacrifice too. She and her household made a public profession of their faith by being baptized together. Lydia continued to demonstrate wisdom in the choices she made for her future. She determined that she would minister to those that led her to the Lord by offering the men a place to stay while they were in town. However, her ministry to open her home to the missionaries was based on one condition: their judgment of her faithfulness to the Lord.

Usually judgment has a negative connotation to it. "Don't judge me" is often times said either before a person does something they aren't proud of or after they have been caught doing something that causes them to be ashamed. Instead of hiding from judgment, Lydia invited it. Based on Lydia's wisdom thus far, I don't believe her statement was pompous. I am convinced that Lydia was genuinely asking the men to critique her so that she would be found faithful in the new life she was living. If she were living in contrast to the teachings of Christ, Lydia was giving the men an opportunity to correct her errant ways.

It is also important to note that Lydia asked the men to judge her based on her faithfulness to the Lord, not their opinion. She made evident that she wanted to live according to God's standards, not mans'. It is imperative that the advice we give or take, the assumptions we make or the doctrine we abide by or preac,h lines up completely with the teachings of Jesus.

Read John 4:6-14.

Through Christ's conversation with the Samaritan woman we learn that each of us has been created to become a vessel for the Lord. Jesus taught this using the illustration of an indwelling well that each of us possesses that was created to be filled with living water. We are given the choice of whether we allow Jesus to fill the well or if we choose to leave it empty. He offers "water springing up into everlasting life". II Peter 2:17 acknowledges that there are those that live as "wells without water". These are people that have chosen to work in contradiction to the Lord. Their end, as well as their teachings, leads to destruction.

Take the opportunity to praise the Lord for the people that you believe to have their well full of the living water. Then list those that you are concerned may be walking through life on empty. Take time to pray for these people and for an opportunity to offer them Christ.

Lydia was wise in recognizing that she didn't know all there was to know about living for Christ. Because she was willing to learn and to grow, she identified people that she deemed trustworthy, people she believed to be vessels of living water, and surrounded herself with them. She then gave them freedom to critique her walk with the Lord in hopes of continuing to be an influential Christian. This is an approach we can model in gaining the Lord's wisdom.

Like Lydia, we need to be conscience of the well that we are drawing from. The missionaries would be held accountable for the assessment they would give Lydia. They could correctly give her an answer only if they used the Word as the measuring tool. Lydia would be responsible for what she did with it. Their answer should only be received as guidance and to give her direction to look deeper into the counsel they provided. It should not be taken as the infallible truth because man has a tendency, whether intentional or not, to become so caught up in their own opinions that they begin to present them as if they are part of the recorded Word.

Choose a conviction that you feel strongly about and write down the scripture that supports that truth. Scripture references not only validate our beliefs, but they also embolden us to more effectively share it with others.

Living Victorious

In Lesson Five: Benefiting From Your Allies, we studied the wisdom of following after wise, mature Christians. Even more critical than learning from the wise is to be able to correctly identify who the wise are. The Word is to be used as our reference point.

The people that are capable of possessing wisdom from the Lord are likened to the bride of Christ (Ephesians 5:25). The last chapter of Proverbs gives us characteristics of a good wife, known as a virtuous woman. These traits should be evident in any wise person that you are intending to seek counsel from or model your life after.

Read Proverbs 31:10-31.

Each of the seven pillars of wisdom is reiterated in this prototype of the church. The wife is sensitive (verse 11), consistent (verse 12) and considers the future (verse 15). She is realistic (verse 16), compassionate (verse 20), prepared (verse 21) and takes personal responsibility (verse 22).

But instead of focusing on the individual pillar, we are going to study what the house built by wisdom looks like from a distance. As a whole, the structure or body of Christ can be described as authentic and diligent. When choosing a mentor these two traits should be an indisputable part of their character.

A wise person understands that they are seen as an extension of Christ. Therefore, they will consistently display Christlike characteristics for all people to see. Within this passage of scripture we are taught that authenticity is expected regardless of who is in our company.

"Her children arise up, and call her blessed; her husband also, and he praiseth her." Proverbs 31:28

Behind closed doors the virtuous woman lived a life that honored the Lord the same way it did in public. In her closest relationships she was seen as a lady that was blessed and worthy of praise. Acknowledging that our flesh needs to be put away at all times can have an enormous impact on those that we consider most valuable to us and also on the way they perceive Christ. Being an authentic person in seclusion trickles into the public life we lead.

However, it is often in the comfort of our own homes that it becomes easiest to fall prey to schemes of Satan. Whether it is because we tire of battling and begin to see our houses as off limits or feel that our poor choices will have less of an impact on God's kingdom, our efforts to be a constant follower of Christ can become slack. But to be an authentic follower of Jesus we need to make decisions that glorify Christ and deny the flesh, even when it is only ourselves or our closest family members that are witness to it.

Read Luke 12:1-3.

Indulging in private sin will eventually hurt your public witness. Now is the time to put an end to something that you only permit in secret. What can you do to become a more authentic follower of Christ?

"Give her of the fruit of her hands; and let her own works praise her in the gates." Proverbs 28:31

The virtuous woman didn't shy away from work. Instead she willingly sought it out (verse

13). She, her family, her neighbors and her employees would reap the benefits of her choices. The motive behind her diligence is given: she wanted to honor the Lord (verse 30).

As Christians we need to remind ourselves that we are to be working out of thankfulness for God's gift that we have promised to us. We all stand in need of a savior and only the blood of Jesus is capable of redeeming us. When we accept that Christ has freely given his life for us, we will be diligent about doing God's will in our life and not tire of following where he leads.

Read Matthew 20:1-16.

The all-day worker felt he deserved more than those that were hired later in the day. This caused him to feel cheated by the master. The worker failed to acknowledge that he was getting exactly what had been promised to him. He chose to ignore that these new workers had been given a great opportunity just as he had been given only hours earlier. The man that was hired first became so fixated on the reward that he failed to respect the employer and his co-workers. As a result, murmurings and dissatisfaction erupted. The worker had allowed his initial gratefulness to the master to be replaced with ingratitude.

Every person, at some point in their life, was once idle. But now we know our purpose: to work for the master. In this parable we see that Jesus is the master that calls us to work for him. His sacrifice isn't weakened based on our circumstances. Therefore, he can offer whomever he pleases entrance into his kingdom at any time. Just as the master promised each worker the same pay, Jesus promises us the same reward: an eternal home in heaven.

The virtuous woman's work ethic is a picture of a contented worker for Christ, unlike the worker in the parable. This wise worker realizes that they received salvation freely and works unto the Lord as a result of the grace they have obtained. Therefore, the work doesn't cause bitterness to spring up within them. Instead, the works are a showing of faith rooted in God's mercy lending itself to legitimizing their walk with the Lord (James 2:17).

Read II Corinthians 9:6-8.

God blesses our efforts when we give of ourselves willingly and cheerfully. Any sense of entitlement is put to rest when we work out of gratitude to glorify God. With this attitude, our works are seen as a labor of love that the Lord honors. Ask the Lord to remind you of a work that you were part of that he blessed. Record it below.

Authenticity and diligence are evidence that a person is serious about serving Christ and should be undeniable in a person that you are looking to learn from. These two characteristics must have been evident in the lives of Paul and his fellow missionaries in order for Lydia to go to them for advice. Prayerfully consider who you can look to for wisdom.

Meeting Three: Victory in Sight

"Through thee will we push down our enemies: through thy name will we tread them under that rise up against us." Psalm 44:5

Set Up for Victory

All Christians have Jesus as their rock solid foundation. How we are building on that rock is based on the decisions we make. I Corinthians 3:10b says "But let every man take heed how he buildeth thereupon." The seven pillars give us an outline of what to work on if we want to build wisely. Some probably stand out to each of us as needing more tending to than others. One that stands out to me is "consistency".

I don't know how many times I have sat down with a daily reading plan for my Bible only to quit after a short time into it. I would get irritated with myself. Falling short to the standards I put on myself wasn't doing much for my self-esteem. I turned to the Lord for direction. He took me away from the pre-made plans I had come up with and led me into the Word in an entirely different way; a way that he knew would work for me. God knows us better than we know ourselves. I didn't need a checklist to be an avid Bible reader. I needed to rely on the Spirit to lead me. Consistency for me, I am learning, doesn't mean that I follow what I think makes most sense but that I continually put my flesh aside to follow Jesus.

Share with the group what pillar you need to really focus on to build a house of wisdom.

Seeing the Field

Uzziah, at a young age, was wise because he sought out God's wisdom. This caused him to be a great leader because he planned to win. He valued land and knew the importance of barriers. As he grew older Uzziah got out of the habit of seeking God's wisdom. This was the downfall of Uzziah's reign.

I gauge the closeness of my relationship with God based on my desire to study the Bible. If I intentionally procrastinate getting into the Word I know that there is something wrong with either my attitude or my obedience. The sooner that I admit that I am distancing myself from the Lord by avoiding the Word, the sooner I can get back on track.

We all have areas that are indicators of how closely we are walking with the Lord. What does that look like for you? What triggers you to think that you need to step back and reevaluate your priorities? It could be your willingness to serve, the way you worship or how intentional you are in glorifying God. Share with the group what part of your routine has the most impact on you.

Perfect Prototype

Jesus left heaven with his purpose in mind: to glorify his father and to make redemption possible for all of mankind. The life that he was led to gave way to him fulfilling that calling. He was given numerous opportunities to glorify God. People came to him for healing. He had the soldiers to approach him in the garden of Gethsemane. His steps were ordered and he was willing to walk the path that God had made for him.

If we look at our lives, most likely we will find that there is something that has been with you for years. The question then becomes: what are you going to do with it?

I have always had the desire to teach. From the time that I was a child I would play the role of teacher and have my sister and brother to be my students. I would spend hours making lesson plans and making work pages for them to do. I loved teaching. I never doubted that I wanted to be a classroom teacher when I grew up.

When I was in high school the Lord began to deal with me about becoming a teacher of his Word. I had a decision to make. Was I going to turn from the path that God had placed me on or would I accept the calling that he had put on my life?

I accepted what the Lord had for me. Soon after I surrendered to teach, I taught my first bible lesson. Since then, as long as I have sought out an opportunity to teach, the Lord has provided for me. The platform may not always be what I have had planned but the Word still gets out.

God has a plan for you. Maybe you are living it out now. Perhaps you are still trying to figure it out. Look at what you are drawn to naturally. If you love to cook, then look for opportunities to share your talent with others. If you like to sing, then make a joyful noise unto the Lord. Share with the group how God is working through you.

The Battle Fought in Solitude

Satan has been named a liar and a murderer (John 8:44). The Son of God has been given the name above all names: Jesus (Philippians 2:9). The people that have surrendered to Christ have been given a name: sons of God (John 1:12). All of these identifiers were given by God himself.

Abraham called God Jehovah-Jireh, The Lord Will Provide (Genesis 22:14). He gave him that name after God provided a ram as a sacrifice in the place of his son Isaac. Moses called God Jehovah-Nissi, The Lord My Banner (Exodus 17:15). He named him that after the Israelites overtook Amalek.

If I were to choose a name to describe who God has been to me, I would call him The Lord My Ever-Patient Teacher. Often times I am slow to grasp the lessons that God is trying to teach me. But the Lord, in all of his patience and love, doesn't quit trying. I am so grateful that he provides me with opportunity after opportunity to learn what he has for me. He doesn't just give me one chance and then give up. When the lessons finally dawn on me, I don't feel condemned.

Convicted? Sometimes, yes. Loved? Always. He shows me where to go from that point, giving me hope and encouragement.

If you were to choose a name to describe something that Jesus has done for you, what would it be?

Benchmark for Success

Lydia had people that she could count on to give her wise counsel. She didn't dismiss that blessing the Lord had presented her with. She chose to call on the men, asking them to help her to grow in Christ. The virtuous woman, a representation of what you and I should be able to be described as, was authentic and diligent about her work in glorifying God. She represented herself and her God well. Both are examples of where we can look to as we march to victory.

In addition to us knowing the scriptures, it is beneficial for us to know who we can turn to for guidance. In Lesson Eleven: Benchmark for Success, you were to list people that you believed to have accepted Christ as their personal savior, those that had their well full of living water. Out of that list there is probably someone you would feel comfortable enough to seek advice from.

From the list I have made, there are a few people that I would willingly turn to for advice. The person that I choose to approach most often is one that doesn't get caught up in emotions. He sees life through the teachings of the Word. The decisions he makes for his family are done with the intentions of glorifying Christ. I watch this person devote his life to serve others, all in the name of Jesus. I am confident that when I go to him for wisdom based on the Word, he will be able to provide it. This person is my husband.

I encourage you to know who you can to turn in times of need. Being only as specific as you'd like to be, share with the group the reasons you give that person permission to have such an enormous impact on your life.

Our God has set us up to win. For us to be a wise warrior we must remember this truth as we battle. The weapon that we have been given will fight for us. The armor that Christ has provided is capable of withstanding any attack. We can battle confidently because we understand that God is for us. In Chapter Four: Our Battle Cry, we are going to be studying how we can share our message of hope and victory with the lost and dying world.

Our Battle Cry

"A good name is rather to be chosen than great riches, and loving favour rather than silver and gold." Proverbs 22:1

Lesson Twelve: Sound the Horn

If we go back to David's story as recorded in I Samuel 18, we see that the wisdom he possesses is highly beneficial to him. It has resulted in a peace for David. God has also given David a firm foundation. David is choosing to build upon it by continually relying on God. He has become known as a great warrior because he always comes back victorious from battles.

Read I Samuel 18:30. How did David conduct himself? What was the result of that?

In the previous chapters of this study we have discussed what wise relationships within the church should look like. We've also studied the wisdom in fighting an internal battle. In this chapter we will be studying the potential to affect the world we live in by submitting to the wisdom of the Lord.

Wisdom Brings Glory to Jesus

God was specific when he gave the Ten Commandments. The children of Israel weren't to bow down or serve any other gods (Exodus 20:1-5). To be wise in the ways of the Lord they needed to respect his commandments. The Israelites needed to be completely devoted to God alone.

King Ahab, leader of Israel, had chosen to forsake God. He erected an altar to sacrifice to Baal. The Israelites followed after his leadership and strayed from the Lord. Elijah, a prophet of the Lord, had a message for Ahab. The Israelites were about to face a drought that would last for years as a consequence of idol worship. There wasn't to be any rain or dew until Elijah called it down from heaven.

Read I Kings 18:17-40.

Elijah had been chosen as God's representative because of his commitment to respect God and his commandments. This, we know, is the cause for Elijah obtaining wisdom from the Lord. Obtaining this heavenly wisdom caused Elijah to have a different lifestyle and viewpoint than the vast majority of the Israelite nation.

Living in contrast to God's Word caused Ahab to rely on worldly wisdom. Ahab's unwillingness to acknowledge God's Word as the law to be followed versus Elijah's determination to live by nothing else caused tension between the two men. Rather than to acknowledge his sin as the cause for the drought, Ahab began to condemn the righteousness of Elijah. These accusations from the leader of the majority didn't weaken Elijah. Instead of being ashamed of his wisdom, he allowed it to be his strength.

Our wisdom shouldn't be hid from the world. It should be what people see. Write about a time when you chose to stand by your wisdom instead of hiding it.

Resolving to live by the wisdom of the Lord set Elijah apart from the people that he was being called to minister to. It also gave him a platform to stand on. He had the attention of the crowd. He spoke with authority because he was speaking on behalf of the Lord. Elijah boldly declared who he was for. He didn't fear the masses, the outcome or the opponent. He had complete peace in standing for the Lord.

When we are relaying God's message we can be bold and at peace because we understand that the Word is the final authority.

Write out John 12:48.

Surrounded by the king, false prophets and the nation of Israel, Elijah challenged God's chosen people to make a decision. The false prophets would be given the opportunity to call on their god, Baal, to consume their sacrifice with fire. Then Elijah would be given the opportunity to call upon his God to consume his sacrifice with fire. Whichever God answered would be the God that they would serve. The people of Israel agreed to the terms.

From morning to evening Baal's prophets begged, pleaded and even cut themselves to gain the attention of their god. They didn't receive any response.

It was now Elijah's turn. He built an altar of the Lord. He prepared the sacrifice. Then he drenched it and the altar in water. Three times he poured water upon it. Elijah wasn't about to back down. Confidence in our Lord, displayed by following his commands, is something that Satan fears because he knows that God will honor it.

Write out Proverbs 2:8.

The altar and sacrifices were soaked. People watched as Elijah began to pray. Elijah acknowledged his God as Lord of Israel; he reiterated that he was his servant and that this was all being done according to the word of the Lord. He then closed his prayer by asking the Lord to use this miracle to turn the nation's hearts back toward God.

Elijah was sure to give God all the glory. He referred to himself as only a servant. The words he said acknowledged that God was the one in control. Elijah had taken every opportunity to make this about the Lord and not himself. He did this because he was fully aware of where the power he possessed came from.

If we are going to live according to the wisdom of the Lord then we should publicly glorify God, talk of his goodness and make his blessings known.

Write out Psalm 105:1-3.

The fire of the Lord fell and consumed not only the sacrifice but also the entire altar. It also licked up the water from the trenches that surrounded it. Then the people fell on their faces and began to worship the Lord God. An entire nation turned back to their God and a three year drought ended because one man was willing to walk wisely when no one else would.

"A little one shall become a thousand, and a small one a strong nation: I the Lord will hasten it in his time." Isaiah 60:22

The Lord can take your personal choice to become a follower of his and use it to impact people in ways you may never know. As his children we are megaphones of his message. We are the people that have been chosen and ordained to live out his gospel and spread his word (John

15:16). When we walk according to his will we are taking his message to the ends of the earth (Acts 1:8). Jesus is being lifted up and in doing so he is drawing people to him (John 12:32).

Lesson Thirteen: Life Preservers

Jesus said in the last part of John 10:10 "I am come that they might have life, and that they might have it more abundantly." Christ's mission becomes our own when we commit to following him. Our mission should be sharing life with the dying world.

Toss It Out

Read I Samuel 25:1-13.

Nabal was an evil man that was rich in worldly goods. He lived in Manon with his wife, Abigail, a wise woman. David and six hundred of his men set up camp nearby in the wilderness of Paran.

David instructed ten of his men to approach Nabal peacefully in hopes of obtaining food and water for their camp. They were to tell Nabal of the kindness and respect that David's men had shown him by the way that they had conducted themselves towards his servants.

Instead of being grateful and generous toward David and his men, Nabal acted selfishly. He refused David's request, claiming that he didn't have any knowledge of who David was. This act of self-centeredness didn't sit well with David. He told his men to get ready for battle. They were going to destroy Nabal and his men.

In this single exchange we learn that Nabal was not seeking direction from the Lord. He was living only for himself. He was so focused on building his empire that he didn't give any care to those around him. Had Nabal been focused on obtaining wisdom from God, he would have noticed this opportunity to use his prosperity to be a blessing to David. This choice would have created a chance for David to glorify God and would have caused Nabal to find favor in David's eyes. It would have also saved Nabal from a pending battle that he was certain to lose. At the root of Nabal's decision to value the treasures of this earth more than the treasures of heaven was his lacking desire to live by the wisdom of God.

Gaining earthly goods isn't a problem unless the acquisition of them comes through denying God's principles. The same is true about holding onto your wealth instead of helping a person that comes to you asking for help (Matthew 5:42). Before you act on a decision you've made, confirm that it's a wise choice by asking yourself if God will be glorified or if you are choosing to toss his principles aside. If Nabal had asked himself this question he would have saved himself, his men and his wife a lot of heartache.

Codi Gandee

Salt Shaker

"Ye are the salt of the earth: but if the salt have lost his savour, wherewith shall it be salted? it is thenceforth good for nothing, but to be cast out, and to be trodden under foot of men." Matthew 5:13

Salt, when used as a preserver, enables the food it contacts extended opportunities to be used for its purpose. Christians, the salt of the earth, are meant to offer life to the people of the world, encouraging them to accept the grace that God has provided for them.

Read I Samuel 25:14-35.

The servants of Nabal feared for their lives. They had learned of Nabal's haughty response to David's request. They understood that they, along with the rest of his household were going to face trouble because of their master's response. They approached Abigail, filled her in on the details and hoped that she would be able to resolve this issue before it was too late. They sought her out as their life preserver.

Tragedies cause people to search for comfort, for answers or for help. Abigail's reputation with these men caused them to believe that she was capable of helping them. We may find ourselves in a position to minister to people that are searching for something they don't have. The Word gives us instructions on reaching out to these people.

Read Psalm 31:1-2.

Like the author of this psalm, we go to the Lord because we know that we can trust him, that he will hear us and that he will be our defense and guide. When someone approaches us with a personal concern we should view it as an opportunity to represent our Heavenly Father, the God that listens to every word we have to say.

Abigail represented God well in that she made time to listen to the men's concern. She was sensitive to their plea. Her willingness to stop and listen showed them that she cared about their outcome. Imagine if she hadn't heard them out. They would have never had an opportunity to come to her again. David and his men would have overtaken them.

We need to be willing to make time to listen to people. In the space below ask the Lord to show you how you normally react when someone comes to you with a personal concern.

Read Psalm 31:10-16.

The psalmist has continued to pour his heart out to the Lord. He tells him that his past has caused him shame, that he doesn't have any friends and that people are looking to kill him. He then acknowledges that his hope and his future are in the Lord's hands. He realizes that there is still time for God to intervene in his enemies' plans. He asks the Lord to fight for him.

Abigail also determined that as long as her servants were alive then there was hope for them. She didn't tell the men that their situation was too far gone. Instead she showed them that she wanted was best for all of them and acted on their behalf. She packed food to take to David as a peace offering.

In addition to listening to people that come to us with concerns, we can fight for them. What that looks like varies in different situations. Perhaps we will be given an opportunity to meet a need that they have. It may be appropriate for us to offer them the hope of Jesus either through scripture or personal testimony. It could be that we offer to pray with them. At minimum, we should let them know that we will pray for them.

Take this opportunity to let the Lord know that you are willing to fight for others. Ask him to show you what that looks like.

Read Psalm 31:19-24.

After much prayer the writer finally reached a place of peace. He moved from despair to the point where he was able to share the hope Jesus had given him with others.

Just like the psalmist had cried out to God, Abigail approached David boldly but without demand. She understood that she and the men were at his mercy. She stayed in his presence until she felt the peace to leave. In this case, her request was granted. She and her household wouldn't need to fear David's army any longer.

The opportunity for us to impact another person's life can begin by simply listening to what is on their mind. Involving yourself in their situation through prayer is the best thing one can do. I encourage you to follow the psalmist and Abigail's lead by not stopping there. Continue to take their situation to the Lord until you have a peace to stop.

Ask the Lord to have the concern weigh heavily on your mind until the issue is resolved. Pray for an opportunity to follow-up with the person who came to you with a need. Is there someone that you could check in with to see how they are doing?

Although Abigail graciously fought for her servants' lives, theirs weren't the only future she was considering. In addition to her plea for her men to be spared, she spoke on behalf of David's reputation. Abigail knew that God had chosen David to prosper as king. She didn't want any scandal to be in his history, including an impulsive act of revenge on her household. She knew that he was a representative of God and that causeless bloodshed wasn't something that he promoted. She reminded David of the potential backlash he would bring himself and his God if he moved forward with his planned attack.

The decisions we make go beyond representing who we are as a person. They reflect the God that we serve too. We need to consider this when we make choices. At the forefront of our mind we should be convinced that our lifestyle lines up with God's righteousness.

David could have dismissed Abigail's wisdom. Instead, he chose to accept it. Record a time that you were about to make the wrong choice but God sent a messenger to cause you to rethink your choice.

Nabal's arrogance was a display of how little he cared for Abigail. The servants' decision to approach Abigail showed the respect they had for her. David recognized Abigail's presence as an act of the Lord God of Israel.

But Abigail didn't allow any of their views to dictate how she responded to the situation at hand. She didn't find her worth in what her husband thought of her. She didn't respect herself because her servants found her deserving. She went to David without knowing that he would claim that she was God's messenger.

Abigail took measures to preserve her own life because she had experienced God's love. She perceived that God was delaying David's attack because he had a future for her. Recognizing God's hand over the situation caused her to set off after David, fighting for the life she hoped to keep.

Abigail fought in the time at hand so that she could reap the benefits in the future. Even if she had been rejected by David she wouldn't have had to wonder if there was more that she could have done. Write about a time in your life when you chose to press forward in the Lord's work even though you could have easily given up. Even if it didn't go as you expected, can you still remember the peace of following through? Draw strength from that the next time you are tempted to quit.

There are many people that we encounter in our lives. Some stand with us, some stand against us. Regardless of their position we need to share the abundant life with them, just as it has been given to us.

Lesson Fourteen: Lord of the Harvest

"I have glorified thee on the earth: I have finished the work which thou gavest me to do." John 17:4

Jesus' ministry on earth was coming to a close. Rather than portraying defeat, Jesus exuded confidence in what he, through his Father, was able to complete. In this lesson we will be studying his teachings on the spreading of the Word and the importance of having a Christ-like mind as we accept the results of it reaching the world.

Seed Sowers

Jesus taught parables on the joy found in the redemption of a single soul. He taught about the happiness the shepherd was filled with when he found his lost sheep (Luke 15:3-6). He told of the joy experienced by the woman who had found her lost coin (Luke 15:8-10). He preached about the eagerness and longing the father had for his son to return home (Luke 15:11-24). Jesus doesn't overlook the individual. Not only does Christ rejoice over one person's redemption, but he uses the individual's commitment to him to grow his kingdom.

"Verily, verily, I say unto you, Except a corn of wheat fall into the ground and die, it abideth alone: but if it die, it bringeth forth much fruit." John 12:24

Living only for your glory is a lonely place because it lacks connection to Christ. For us to live with the intention of being fruitful for Jesus we must decide to die out to our flesh and surrender to the will of our Lord. There is rejoicing in heaven when a person chooses to live for Christ (Luke 15:10). Angels aren't the only ones to take notice of our salvation. Here on earth our redemption leads to the redemption of others.

We may never know the name of the person that we, because of our relationship with Christ, have had an eternal effect on. However, Jesus assures us that our works aren't in vain. You are the light in this dark world. Write out Isaiah 60:1-2.

Jesus knew that he wouldn't be accepted by everyone. He told us that only a few would enter in at the straight gate (Matthew 7:13-14). But to Jesus, those few would be worth the life he lived and the death he died. The small group of souls that would accept him as their father was worth the rejection that he would face from the masses.

Read Mark 4:1-9 and 13-20.

Through this parable Jesus taught that our results would be the same as he experienced. Even though we, as sowers of the seed, spread the Word faithfully it doesn't always take root. Jesus didn't fault the sower. He didn't link the sower's method to the person's reaction. Instead, he expounded upon the condition of the people's hearts as to why they either rejected or accepted the Word.

Some of the people stood on stony ground, some stood surrounded by thorns, but there were a few that stood on primed land, ready for the Word to become fruitful. Without question, this parable teaches on the reasons why the masses reject Christ versus the few that choose to accept him. In addition to that, this parable can be looked at as a picture of the individual souls and the longsuffering that Christians must possess in hopes of reaching them.

A person faces changing circumstances throughout their lifetime. The people we are surrounded by and environments we live in aren't stagnant. This affects our perception of the world and also our reception of the Word into our lives.

For example, a person reading the story of Noah building the ark may be living in the same wickedness that caused God to want to destroy all the earth. That person may decide that they'd be content riding out the flood rather than hoping to find grace in the eyes of God. Later, that same person may walk through a period of life seeking protection and peace. At that point they may view the same passage of scripture differently and choose to find comfort in the shelter of God, just as Noah found safety in the shelter of the ark.

What scripture has taken on different meaning to you because your situation has changed? In the space below, contrast the differences in your life that has caused you to view the scripture differently.

Jesus' teaching on the parable of the sower illustrates the softening of an individual soul. This individual was worth the life of Christ. Therefore, we shouldn't deny the leading of the Spirit to witness to them just because they have rejected the gospel in the past. People change. Hearts soften. We don't know where that person has been, what they are dealing with now, nor what future our Lord has in store for them. Be patient with the person. Be willing to be gracious because of the grace you have found (II Peter 3:18).

What was the time frame in which you first heard about Jesus and then became fruitful for him?

We are to be encouraged that even though the odds aren't in our favor to win millions to Christ, that being part of the effort that wins one soul for him is worth celebrating. Therefore we must always strive to be found blameless and perfect, living a life that points to Christ (Matthew 5:48).

Reapers of the Ripe

"And herein is the saying true, One soweth, and another reapeth." John 4:35

Of course Jesus wasn't discussing crop production. In the following piece of scripture we see that he used similarities of harvest time to teach us about the need for us to be fixed on the things of his kingdom, the reason Christians should work together and how there is joy for everyone that takes part (Colossians 3:2, I Corinthians 3:9, III John 1:4).

Read John 4:31-38.

Jesus had been traveling from Judea to Galilee by way of Samaria. It was here that he met a woman at a well and revealed himself to her as the Christ. She then went into the city testifying of her experience with the Lord. The result of this was many people coming to hear Jesus speak, just as the disciples were making it back from a trip to the city.

The people that had come to gather around Jesus were like-minded with him in that they were tending to the spiritual matter at hand. The disciples were of a different mindset. In that moment, even though they were attempting to do a good thing by caring for the body of Christ, they were missing the best thing: sharing Christ with others.

Jesus refused the disciples offer of food as an example for us all to learn from. In that act, Jesus taught that our purpose on earth is greater than a goal to make it from one day to the next. The drive within us shouldn't be to live a long life; it should be to share eternal life through Christ with others. When faced with a decision between satisfying the natural and living for the spiritual, wisdom always chooses the spiritual.

As Christians we need to remember that we don't live to please the flesh. We live to do the will of Jesus. In the space below write out Matthew 16:24.

Jesus then directed the disciples' attention to the crowd of people that were looking to him for salvation. He likened the situation to a crop that was ready to be harvested. The seed had been sown by the Samaritan woman who had shared her testimony of Christ. It had fallen upon good ground and taken root in these people's lives. Jesus explained that the disciples were being given the opportunity to reap the rewards of her work by witnessing them come to him for salvation.

However, the disciples had boxed themselves into only working their own field. They had decided that their sole purpose of the time was to care for Jesus' mortal body by feeding him. It became all that they were willing to do. Jesus had them to open their eyes to the crop that was ready to be harvested outside of the field they were working in.

If we aren't careful we can put that same type of limitation on ourselves. We can get so caught up in reaching only a certain type of people or only sharing Jesus through a certain venue, that we miss the opportunity of sharing Christ with those that are staring us in the face. It happened with the disciples; it could easily happen to us.

Through this scripture Jesus makes it clear that even though we might not have any intentions of reaping where another person has sown, we should be willing to act on every opportunity to share the gospel. Working for the Lord should override any stipulations that we create. Harvesting souls is a group effort that the Lord blesses with increase (I Corinthians 3:7).

In the space below ask the Lord to open your eyes to the harvest around you, not just the ones that are part of the field you are sowing in.

If we open our eyes to God's plan for harvesting souls, we will all rejoice when a soul is saved because we understand that it is Jesus' kingdom that is growing. Our style, our personal convictions, our approach isn't what wins people to the Lord. Salvation only comes through the blood of Jesus. However, Christ will use our individuality to reach the masses. Even though we differ in opinions, personalities, cultures, etc., we are one in Jesus (I Corinthians 3:8). It is important that we don't become jealous or prideful of the way the Lord chooses to work through his children.

In the space below list two churches in your area that differ from one another. In addition to Jesus, what stands out to you about those churches? Is it the clothing they wear? The music they listen to? The way the pastor preaches the message? Or how many services they have per week? Now look at the congregation: there is one. God has used that group of people's individuality to reach the people that are filling their seats. There is joy in knowing that the Lord has used someone, even if it wasn't you, to save their souls from Hell.

Our Lord sees what we aren't able to see. He knows what each person's heart looks like and wants them to be his regardless of that fact. We, as his workers, are called to preach the Word, to be a tool that the Lord uses to bring souls to him. The next lesson we will study how we are to go about reaching the world.

Lesson Fifteen: The Message

"The law of the Lord is perfect, converting the soul: the testimony of the Lord is sure, making wise the simple." Psalm 19:7

Our God wants us to be strengthened by his presence (Isaiah 41:10). Reminders of God's provision, protection and even judgment surround us. They are for our benefit. They are tokens encouraging us to boldly live the life that he has called us to.

The Lord used the stars to promise Abraham that his lineage would be great (Genesis 15:1-5). As he fathered child after child, the stars in the night sky served as a reminder to Abraham that God was making good on his promise. Joshua was told to have a memorial of twelve stones to be placed at the bank of the Jordan River to serve as a reminder of the people's passing through it on dry ground (Joshua 4:1-9). Generation after generation would be able to look at the stones as a reminder of God's power. The Israelites were told to sew blue fringes on their clothes as a reminder to not sin against the Lord (Numbers 15:37-40). In each of these instances the Lord spoke to the people out of his love for them. Recognition of his love for them was the reason they loved God.

Just like memorials and reminders were prominent in the days before Jesus walked the earth, God has continued to ordain rituals that would serve as reminders. The Lord's Supper was instituted to serve as a reminder of the love God has for us and of what Jesus did (Luke 22:19-20). God showed his love for us by giving Jesus to be our sacrifice and to become our way for eternal life (John 3:16). Each time we partake in this act of remembrance we are reminded of God's sacrifice, victory and grace that we have obtained. The bread represents his body, broken for us; the cup symbolizing the blood (I Corinthians 11:24-25). Our love for Christ is of the same origin that the Israelites had for the Father. I John 4:19 simply states "we love him, because he first loved us."

Before Jesus came to earth, perhaps the greatest tangible object used to represent God's presence was the Ark of the Covenant. The actual ark embodied the strength of God. Interestingly, there was a section within the Ark of the Covenant that held three items. These items were placed there to testify of God's provision, protection and judgment (Hebrews 9:4). Therefore, the Ark of the Covenant is also sometimes referred to as the Ark of the Testimony (Exodus 26:34).

According to Hebrews 9:4 what three items filled the Ark of the Testimony?

Provision

Read Exodus 16.

The Israelites had just come out from under Egyptian rule. Near the onset of their journey they had already begun to doubt God's provision for them. Murmurings of returning to their former way of life as well-fed slaves started to surface. Their concern for starvation was legitimate. There wasn't a surplus of food surrounding them. They needed the Lord to care for them.

God provided. Six out of the seven days a week the Lord would miraculously provide manna from heaven to feed the Israelite people as they wandered in the wilderness. The seventh day they were told to rest and eat the surplus of manna that had been provided for them the day before. This went on for forty years.

At one point in the midst of that time frame, the Lord commanded Moses to gather a small sample of the manna to place in a pot, serving as a reminder of what God had provided for them. This manna would preserve itself for years to come so that there would be a physical testimony for future generations to look upon and remember God's provision in their great time of need.

Think of a time that the Lord has fulfilled a need of yours. I encourage you to get some type of an object to symbolize that need being met. Maybe that looks like the stub of an electric bill that was paid on time or a picture of a person that God placed in your life. Put it in a place that you can go to the next time you're trusting God to provide for you. What is it that you will use as a remembrance of God's provision in your life?

Protection

Read Numbers 16 and 17.

Jealousy had taken root in Korah's heart. He felt that neither he nor the men that he had persuaded to revolt with him needed Moses and Aaron as their leaders. He accused them of self-anointing, as though God had not chosen them to lead the Israelite people.

Moses, distraught by the accusation but knowing exactly who to turn to, asked the Lord to show the entire congregation that they had been ordained by God and not by their own power. Soon after, Korah and the others that opposed Moses and Aaron died in an earthquake, signifying that God was in control of the leadership of the people.

The Israelites that witnessed this began to murmur against Moses and Aaron, accusing them of murdering Korah and his company. Eventually God decided to settle the matter by having each of the twelve tribes choose a rod to go before the Lord. Each rod would have the name of the tribe's leader written on it. The tribe of Levi, from which Moses and Aaron descended, would have Aaron's name on it. The rod that would blossom would signify who God had chosen to be set apart for the Lord. Aaron's rod bloomed. This was enough to convince the people that God ordained Moses and Aaron as the leaders of the nation.

In future instances when the people began to murmur, Moses would bring out the bloomed rod to remind the people that no one will overthrow God's plan. Aaron's rod was significant because it served as a reminder that God was greater than the enemy.

The blossomed rod would be preserved. The Lord chose to have it set aside as a reminder that the rebels, those that went against God's chosen people, wouldn't stand. God had it placed with the Ark of the Testimony.

In the space below record Revelation 3:8.

The Word teaches that as Christians we will face tribulations and afflictions (I Thessalonians 3:3-4). These aren't reasons for us to waiver in our faith. Instead we should continue to trust the Lord by living according to his Word. Just as God didn't allow Korah and the men to shut the door on Moses and Aaron's role within the Israelite nation, no one possesses the power to close the door on what God has set you up for.

We all partake in spiritual warfare. Some battles are more intense than others. Some take on more of a significant meaning to us. If you can, recall a time when you know that the Lord fought on your behalf. Ask the Lord to show you what keepsake could be used to represent that difficult time. Put it alongside the item that reminds you of God's provision for your life. What did you choose to remind yourself that God is your protection?

Judgment

Read Exodus 31:18, 32:15-19 and 34:1-35.

Moses climbed Mount Sinai to meet with God. It was here that Moses would receive the two tables of stone that would have the laws written upon them. These laws were the standard in which the people would be judged.

As Moses climbed down from the mountain he heard noises. Upon his return to the congregation of people he found them worshipping a golden calf. In anger, Moses threw the two tables of stone on the ground, crushing the tablets.

Later, God had Moses to make the trek back up the mountain with a second set of stones. The Lord had Moses rewrite the commandments making these two tables identical to the first set.

The purpose of these laws was to set the people apart from all other people (Exodus 19:5-6). Record in the space below I Peter 2:9.

We have been set apart because of the mercy that we have obtained through Jesus (I Peter 2:10). Jesus is now the standard of life. He is the fulfillment of the law. He is the reason we will be able to stand at the last Day of Judgment and be given entrance into the kingdom of heaven.

It's only because of Christ that we have a testimony to share. Always, for every Christian, we should remind ourselves of our need for God's redemption in our life. For every follower of Christ, Jesus is the "table of stones" that reminds us of judgment that we will face with him and enter into heaven because of him.

God's judgment will not be avoided by anyone (Psalm 96:13). Therefore our need for Christ's atonement for our sin should be shared with people so that they, too, will be prepared to stand before God.

Think back to the time that you accepted Christ as your Savior. What comes to mind? The scripture? The place? The person that led you to him? The time of day? Signify that memory with something you can touch. Put it with the other two items. In the space below write down what you have chosen.

The significance of the three items within the Ark of the Testimony is a starting point for us to be able to easily recount our testimony of God's presence in our life. Throughout this lesson you have gathered items that have special meaning to you to use as reminders of God's provision, protection and judgment for you. What you have compiled is a condensed version of your own testimony to share with the world.

The Ark of the Covenant was a testimony to the people of Israel. It was the vessel of God created to remind his people of his involvement in their past, to encourage them in their present time and to strengthen their trust in him for their future.

Like the Ark of the Testimony, followers of Christ are chosen vessels of God. Just as the items in the ark spoke to the people of Israel, our lives are a testimony to the people around us. Your own testimony is of the Lord. It is worthy to be shared.

Am I a Hypocrite?

Occasionally we back away from sharing our testimony. For some of us, we wrestle with accepting the grace of God for fear of being labeled as another hypocrite in the church. We are plagued with the question of "this is too good to be true, right?" This is a common battle that many Christians fight. The Word teaches on the differences between a recipient of grace and a church-going hypocrite.

Peter was a well known disciple of Christ. He had left his previous life as a fisherman to follow after Jesus (Matthew 4:18-20). When Jesus asked who Peter thought he was, he responded "Thou art the Christ, the Son of the living God." (Matthew 16:16). Peter was one of the men that Jesus took with him up the mountain for the transfiguration (Matthew 17:1-2). On the eve of Christ's crucifixion Peter asked the Lord to wash not only his feet but his head and hands as well, signifying he was completely committed to Jesus (John 13:9). No one could deny that Peter was a committed follower of Christ.

Yet, in a moment of weakness, he denied knowing the Lord three different times. He had crumbled under pressure. Peter was overwhelmed with shame, weeping when he realized what he had done (Matthew 26:69-75).

After Jesus rose from the grave he went to his disciples, including Peter. He didn't condemn Peter as hypocritical. Instead, he extended him the opportunity to continue to build the kingdom of God (John 21:15).

Be sure to take notice that Peter hadn't faltered just once. He spoke impulsively and acted quickly on a few different occasions. He was the one that suggested that three tabernacles be built on the mountain after the transfiguration of Christ (Matthew 17:4). He was in the group that fell asleep instead of praying like Jesus had asked them to do (Mark 14:32-38). Peter was the man that cut off the soldier's ear in the Garden of Gethsemane (John 18:10).

Satan would have us to believe that God doesn't want someone that has done wrong to come to him for a second chance, or a third, or however many. But this is a lie. God's grace is always available to the repentant heart.

However, there were people that Jesus interacted with that had no intentions of repentance. These were the scribes and Pharisees that intentionally exploited God for their own benefit. They mistreated widows for their own gain, under the pretense of serving God. They converted people to their religion, which they claimed was based on God's law. In doing so they convinced people to follow after their methods instead of God's law (Matthew 23:14-15). Jesus said to them "Woe unto you, scribes and Pharisees, hypocrites!"

Jesus sees our actions and hears our words. He knows if we are repentant or if we are unremorseful. Not everyone will believe the power of God's grace, but that doesn't have to hinder you from receiving it. God is the judge of your soul. People's opinions don't affect what he has done for you and they aren't reason for us to deny our call to share the goodness of God. Now is the day of salvation (II Corinthians 6:2). Today is the time to share our testimony. We are responsible for getting the message out.

Lesson Sixteen: Field Workers

"Is it not yet a very little while, and Lebanon shall be turned into a fruitful field, and the fruitful field shall be established as a forest? And in that day shall the deaf hear the words of the book, and the eyes of the blind shall see out of obscurity, and out of darkness." Isaiah 29:17-18

In this lesson we will continue to work with the parables in Lesson Fourteen: Lord of the

Harvest, by combining the two analogies. As followers of Jesus, the Lord of the harvest, we become workers in the field. We are going to study different ways we should be sowing the seed in the field that has yet to be harvested, or in plain terms, sharing Jesus with the people of the world that have yet to accept Christ.

The strength we possess to be field workers comes only through the acceptance of Jesus' sacrifice and the self-denial to follow after his leading (Matthew 16:24). Part of wisdom is to understand that the power-filled tool that we have been given to reach the harvest is our testimony (Acts 1:8). Our personal experience with Christ is so influential that it, paired with the working of the Holy Spirit, has the potential to cause the spiritually deaf to hear and the spiritually blind to see. Therefore, we have the responsibility of sharing the gospel by speaking of our faith and displaying it through our actions (Matthew 28:19).

The workers in the field are identifiable by their words and actions. I Thessalonians 5:14-15 gives a summary of how Christians should interact with those around them. List them in the space below.

Something to Hear

Read Mark 5:25-34.

Figuratively speaking, this woman was standing in the field, not yet a follower of Christ. She was seeking after a physical healing in hopes of it leading her to wholeness. Yet here she was, disappointed and still searching. This woman was living life without any regard to Jesus.

But then we read of her gratitude towards him as she falls at his feet, healed of her disease. The words that Jesus spoke to her tell us about the change that had overcome the woman in his presence.

He acknowledged that she had put her faith in him. It made her whole, filling with living water the well that had once been dried. He told her that she could live peaceably now; no longer searching, but rather content with what she had found in him: both a physical and spiritual healing.

Why then would she have waited twelve years before she approached Jesus? Mark 5:27 records the action that caused the woman to seek Christ. Write in the space below what prompted her to go to Jesus.

Her life changed when she heard about Jesus. Someone, either directly or indirectly, had shared a testimony of a personal experience with Christ that convinced this woman to consider him worthwhile. The words resonated within her so deeply that she determined to go to Jesus with her desire to be made whole.

Consider the fact that you may be the chosen vessel to reach a lost soul. I Thessalonians 2:4 states "But as we were allowed of God to be put in trust with the gospel, even so we speak; not as pleasing men, but God, which trieth our hearts."

Your spoken salvation story is referred to as a "word of faith" (Romans 10:8). Sharing your testimony could be the cause for another person to place their faith in Christ. With the intention of praiseworthy reflection and as an act of preparation, write in the space below your salvation story.

Something to See

As wonderful as it is for a person to come to Christ at the first mention of him, it doesn't always work that way. We know that Jesus doesn't want anyone to perish. That is why he came to provide us the perfect sacrifice: his sinless self as atonement for our sin. But, for some, the decision to come to Christ is hard-won. This had been the case for Saul of Tarsus.

Saul knew the Jewish religion. He told of his zeal for the tradition (Galatians 1:14). He admitted that he attempted to destroy people's faith in Christ and tried to prevent anyone from calling on Jesus as their Lord (Galatians 1:23). He was intent on persecuting Christians. He would break into houses to arrest men and women for worshipping Christ (Acts 8:3). During all of this, he was hearing of Christ and watching Jesus' followers live and die in his name.

In Lesson Seven: Set Up for Victory, we read about a man named Stephen. Stephen preached a sermon about the Jewish history and the crucifixion of Christ. Saul was in attendance for that message. He orchestrated the execution of Stephen. Stephen had spoken of Jesus and showed his faith in Christ as he praised God while they were stoning him.

In spite of the hatred and contempt Saul had for Christ, Jesus continued to pursue Saul. He wanted Saul to be one of his adopted children, a vessel for him. Our Lord is longsuffering, or patient, as he tries to win us over to him (II Peter 3:9). We shouldn't experience anger or annoyance while following our Savior's lead (Colossians 1:11). Referencing Colossians 1:11 what should our patience be mixed with?

Part of wisdom is to recognize that a spiritual battle for the soul is a fight that we should see through to the end. As long as a person has breath then we should be joyous that they still have opportunity to accept Christ as their savior. We should be willing and ready to share our testimony in any way possible to any person that we are led to.

Read Acts 9:1-20.

Presently Ananias was serving Christ faithfully among his brethren. Now he was being asked to demonstrate his faith in front of a person that was known for rejecting the gospel. Jesus didn't tell Ananias to send word to Saul confirming the experience he had on Damascus Road. The Lord's direction for Ananias was clear: Go to Saul in my name and lay your hands on him. If Ananias was obedient he would be showing a great display of his faith in the Lord with these actions. However, his initial response was a mix of fear and contempt. Saul had persecuted Ananias' spiritual brethren, people living the very lifestyle he had adopted. Had you or I been in the same situation, our reaction to the vision may have been similar to Ananias'.

The radical act of a Christian coming to assist in the receiving of his sight wouldn't be lost on Saul. He understood that this would be a testimony to the goodness of Jesus. Thankfully, Ananias' initial response of hesitation, doubt and reasons to stay put didn't outweigh his final decision. Ananias made the best of this opportunity and demonstrated his devotion to Christ by following him out of his comfort zone. Because of Ananais' showing of faith, Saul received not only his earthly vision but his blinded eyes were open to see spiritually as well. Saul had finally accepted Christ for who he is.

The redemption of Saul had been a long time coming. Ananias wasn't the only person to live a life of faith for to Saul to see. He just happened to be the one that witnessed Saul's transformation.

You are not alone in the field. Surrounding you are laborers that are focused on the same goal. Part of our work is to ask the Lord to continue to send people to help us labor. Another part of our workload is to continue to pray for ourselves and fellow Christians that we will be diligent and authentic workers for him. If we are going to preach the Word then we need to be found living the Word as well.

Record in the space below I Corinthians 9:14.

As workers for Christ we can become discouraged about sharing the gospel with others. The fear we experience should never sway our work for the Lord. I Corinthians 13:12 says "For now we see through a glass, darkly; but then face to face: now I know in part; but then shall I know even as also I am known." The unknown is a part of reality that God is present in. It isn't a place for us to put faith in ourselves; it is an opportunity for us to trust God while sharing our faith with others.

Our decisions are impactful to those that are listening to us speak and watching the way we live. When the Spirit moves on you to speak, do it; even when you think sharing your testimony will be to no benefit. Be willing to show up for Christ because there is significance in being present. Jesus says that where two or three are gathered in his name, he is there in the midst of them (Matthew 18:20). We should always be found living in obedience to Christ's leading no matter how outlandish it may seem. Lost souls are at stake and they are worth our attention.

Meeting Four: Our Battle Cry

"A good name is rather to be chosen than great riches, and loving favour rather than silver and gold." Proverbs 22:1

Sound the Horn

Elijah's life glorified God. His willingness to stand and proclaim the goodness of God impacted an entire nation of people. His boldness to live for the Lord didn't go unnoticed.

People that have gone on before us or maybe even certain people that we are currently walking through life with, can have an enormous impact on how we view Jesus. Everyone has at least one person that they can point to that has helped to shape their relationship with Christ. Many of us are blessed to have a few people in our lives that have made a difference.

For me, one of those people was my Great-Grandma Faith. I remember, as a child, walking into her classroom as she was teaching a Sunday School lesson. I just stopped and stared in awe. I can't remember what she was teaching on but I do remember the complete authority, yet softness, she spoke with. The entire room seemingly hung to her every word. This experience, mixed in with the obvious love, respect and admiration that my mom had for her, made me want to take notice of how she lived. I watched her live in a way that let you know, without a doubt, that she was completely devoted to the Lord and to the cause of living a life that led others to Christ. I am so grateful for the presence that Grandma Faith has had on my life.

Tell about a person that has had a positive effect on your life because of the way they have brought glory to Jesus.

Life Preservers

Abigail's mentality saved herself, her husband and her workers. Her wisdom encouraged David to continue to walk in the ways of the Lord. Abigail was a fighter and the people around her could see it.

Earlier I mentioned that my family and I left our home to move hours away to a place that we felt certain God was calling us to. When we left that area we left behind our current lifestyle. Like I said, I had been responsible for preparing three lessons a week. I was in the Word a lot. The first eighteen months after the move I had almost zero responsibility of preparing a lesson. The lack of responsibility to teach led me to believe that the study of the Word wasn't as important anymore. My routine of Bible study diminished.

Eventually I came to the realization that I wasn't doing any favors for myself by omitting Bible study. I was at a place of brokenness and shame when I realized that I had allowed what had once been a large part of my routine to become almost non-existent.

I remember calling my sister to share with her what I had finally acknowledged. She didn't downplay what I had come to her with. Instead, she fought for me. In addition to listening to my story, she asked if I would like to do a Bible study with her. She said that we could discuss each lesson every day. She was going to hold me accountable. That's what we did.

Since that period of time I have continued to grow because Bible study has once again become a large part of my Christian walk. To this day, if I notice my want to get into the Word slipping, I know that I need to go to the Lord in prayer and that my sister is willing to go there with me.

Share with the group a person that has come alongside you to help fight your battle.

Lord of the Harvest

In the parable of the sower the heart of the person that was hearing the message changed over time.

"A new heart will I give you, and a new spirit will I put within you: and I will take away the stony heart out of your flesh, and I will give you an heart of flesh." Ezekiel 36:26

I am so grateful that my once stony heart has now transformed into a heart that will receive the message God has for me.

Before I had accepted Christ as my savior I remember feeling anger towards the men that waited until the last moment to come to Christ in the parable of the laborers. I looked at my aunt while the sermon was being preached and whispered, "I get why those early morning workers were mad. I'd be mad too."

She said "Well Codi Brown!" She went on to explain what Jesus was teaching, "You should always be happy for people that decide to follow Jesus."

Now I look at that piece of scripture the same way my aunt does, through eyes of grace. Instead of seeing a person that was cheating at life, I now see a person that barely escaped an eternity in Hell. I realize now that grace is needed by everyone, including those that come to Christ at a young age. To be a recipient of grace, no matter what stage of life you are in, is worth rejoicing over.

When I study that particular passage I have joy knowing that there is still hope for a person as long as they're living. I have learned that this time on earth is a preparation for eternity and that our will should be like the Father's, in which no one should perish but that we all would gain eternal life.

Studying the scriptures takes on an entirely different perspective once a person is saved. Share with the group an example of how your perspective has changed since you've accepted the Lord as your savior.

The Message

Psalm 124:1 says "If it had not been the Lord who was on our side, now may Israel say;" It goes on to describe the differences of outcome they would have experienced. This verse can easily be made personal by replacing Israel with your name.

Generally speaking, we can say that he saved me from Hell or that he gave me breath. But specifically, what has happened that you can point to as a clear example of his presence in your life?

As mentioned before, my small family moved away from our comfortable, secure life to live in a place that was unknown to us. We had the peace of the Lord to go forward with our decision. However, the way that the entire move played out is something our family looks to for assurance and confidence.

My husband and I decided to have our entire house packed and then sent the moving truck on its way. This wouldn't have been a big deal except we still owned the house that we had just packed up and the new house wasn't yet ours. The realtor tried to discourage us from making this decision but we had to either do it then or wait another three months before moving.

A few mornings later we sold our old home and that afternoon we bought the new one. Our truckload pulled into our new driveway that same day.

I keep a house key as a testimony to God's provision for our family. He called us to this area. He provided a place for us to live and a couple to buy the old home from us. The timing of it all is evidence to us that the move was ordained and blessed by the Lord.

What could you testify to? How has God's presence affected your life? Choose an item from your own testimony to share with the group.

Field Workers

"Therefore said he unto them, The harvest truly is great, but the labourers are few: pray ye therefore the Lord of the harvest, that he would send forth labourers into his harvest." Luke 10:2

The Lord reaches the lost with our efforts to speak of him and to live according to the Word. The lost aren't the only ones affected by the messages being preached. He also strengthens the people that we are working alongside. Observing another worker do the will of God can be very encouraging.

My brother and sister-in-law felt it was the Lord's will for them to accept a position fourteen hours away from their home. Before they moved away they stood before their church and thanked them for the foundation that they had gained because of the seeds that the church had sown in their lives. My brother said "We're going to keep building on it."

I have witnessed them live out those words. They are now into their second year in their new home. They are an active part in their local church. They are choosing to live boldly for God's glory on a daily basis.

They had spoken of what the Lord had done for them and now they are showing their world how God's love and guidance can affect a person. I am so grateful that they have given me something to hear and to see. It has done my heart good.

Share with the group how someone has sown a seed into your life.

The enemy will try to silence God's soldiers. But as long as there are warriors that seek after the wisdom of God, the message of hope and grace will continue to be spread. Join forces with those around you to be bold in sharing your testimonies of the Lord's goodness. A position on the winning side is for anyone that is willing to seek the wisdom from above.

CONCLUSION

The Word of God is full of wisdom. This sixteen lesson study touches on the wisdom that we stand to gain if we continue to seek out the Lord.

I have compiled a condensed list as a quick reference guide for you, highlighting what the Lord has shown me through the study of the Word.

- There is wisdom in accepting that you are in spiritual warfare.
- Obtaining wisdom gives you a Godly peace.
- The wise spiritual warrior will:
    - Invest in God-glorifying relationships.
    - Prioritize their relationship with God.
    - Participate in ministry.
    - Build their lives upon the Word.
    - Seek to glorify God in every area of their life.
    - Judge themselves upon the Word, not the opinions of people.
    - Accept the Word as the final authority.
    - Seek to glorify God.
    - Try to help others make God-glorifying choices.
    - Give precedence to the spiritual matters; not the natural.
    - Acknowledge God's presence in their life.
    - Battle for Jesus.

In conclusion, remember, the wise warrior determines to follow Jesus. Wisdom is paired with peace, frightens Satan and glorifies God. We are victorious in this life and in eternity when we depend on God's wisdom to protect us, to steady us as we battle and share the gospel of Christ. We learn wisdom through the prompting of the Spirit and the study of the Word. Surrendering ourselves to resort to God's teachings versus our own ideas takes initiative and determination. However, in this context, surrendering doesn't mean that we give up; it means we are winning.

Printed in the United States
By Bookmasters